NOW!
CLASSROOMS
GRADES 3–5

**LESSONS FOR ENHANCING
TEACHING AND LEARNING
THROUGH TECHNOLOGY**

MEG ORMISTON

Sheri DeCarlo   **Grace Kowalski**
Sonya Raymond   **Justin Gonzalez**

Solution Tree | Press

a division of
Solution Tree

555 North Morton Street
Bloomington, IN 47404
800.733.6786 (toll free) / 812.336.7700
FAX: 812.336.7790

email: info@SolutionTree.com
SolutionTree.com

Visit **go.SolutionTree.com/technology** to download the free reproducibles in this book.

Printed in the United States of America

21   20   19   18   17   1   2   3   4   5

Library of Congress Cataloging-in-Publication Data

Names: Ormiston, Meghan J., author.
Title: NOW classrooms, grades 3-5 : lessons for enhancing teaching and
   learning through technology / Meg Ormiston, Sheri DeCarlo, Sonya Raymond,
   Grace Kowalski, and Justin Gonzalez.
Description: Bloomington, IN : Solution Tree Press, [2018] | Series: NOW
   classrooms | Includes bibliographical references and index.
Identifiers: LCCN 2017019999 | ISBN 9781945349409 (perfect bound)
Subjects: LCSH: Education, Elementary--Computer-assisted instruction. |
   Educational technology--Study and teaching (Elementary) | School
   improvement programs.
Classification: LCC LB1028.5 .O69 2017 | DDC 371.33--dc23 LC record available at https://lccn.loc.
gov/2017019999

Solution Tree
Jeffrey C. Jones, CEO
Edmund M. Ackerman, President

Solution Tree Press
President and Publisher: Douglas M. Rife
Editorial Director: Sarah Payne-Mills
Art Director: Rian Anderson
Managing Production Editor: Caroline Cascio
Senior Production Editor: Tara Perkins
Senior Editor: Amy Rubenstein
Copy Editor: Jessi Finn
Proofreader: Kendra Slayton
Text and Cover Designer: Rian Anderson
Editorial Assistants: Jessi Finn and Kendra Slayton

To my home team, my husband, Brian, and my sons, Danny and Patrick; and to my first teacher and number-one cheerleader, my mom, Marta Hart.

—MEG ORMISTON

To my husband, David, and my daughters, Samantha and Allison, who have been my inspiration, encouragement, and support throughout the years.

—SHERI DECARLO

To my wonderful husband, Matt, who encouraged me to dare to change on the road to achieving my dreams!

—SONYA RAYMOND

To my number-one supporters Joel, Adrienne, Billy, Ari, and Brad for always believing in me and to Chad Hill, the teacher who taught me everything I know!

—GRACE KOWALSKI

To my family, Guadalupe, Jaime, Jessica, and Julie for the continuous support with everything I do.

—JUSTIN GONZALEZ

Acknowledgments

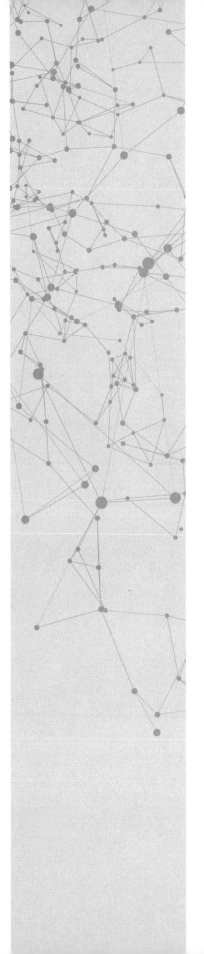

Thank you to all teachers everywhere! I am proud to say I am a teacher, and I believe it is one of the most important professions in the world. Specifically, I want to thank the collaborative writing team that coauthored this series of five books. I have never worked with a more dedicated, fun-loving, collaborative team of lifelong learners. Thanks to the Otus team for your support and to my family for putting up with our writing marathons. I give my deepest thanks to Douglas Rife and the entire team at Solution Tree for helping all of us craft this dream into a reality. Wow!

—Meg Ormiston

My most sincere thanks and appreciation to the teachers and staff with whom I have worked side by side for including me as part of your never-ending desire to bring amazing learning experiences to all students; to the many administrators for your guidance and encouragement to think out of the box and take risks; to the students for bringing your eagerness and excitement for learning to the classroom each day; and to my family for supporting and encouraging me each step of the way, each of whom has played a vital part in supporting and guiding my incredible journey as an educator.

—Sheri DeCarlo

Thank you to my family and friends who have always supported and encouraged my love for teaching! I am so thankful for all the wonderful teaching role models I have had over the years who have provided examples of embracing change, trying new things, and putting kids first. Thank you to all my students who put up with change at a moment's notice as we committed together to doing what is best now and not waiting for the next year. I am truly blessed!

—Sonya Raymond

Thank you to all my students and their families who have brought love, fun, and excitement to each day in my career. Thank you to all my colleagues and administrators who encouraged me to share my story and challenged me to keep pushing myself. Thank you to Jordan Garrett for your mentorship and for being my constant source of inspiration. Thank you to my family and friends, who have supported me in all my adventures and believed in the number-one rule: have fun every day!

—Grace Kowalski

Thank you to my friends and family who have always supported and encouraged me throughout my teaching career. Thank you to one of my former principals, Jeremy Majeski, for believing in me and pushing me to take risks in the classroom and in life. Thank you to every colleague I've had along the way; I have truly learned something from each and every one of you. Thank you to my partner, Sandro Murillo, for always being there and challenging or supporting my ideas. And to all the students who have had an impact on me and my teaching career, thank you for your creativity and innovative ideas each and every day. I've truly learned the most from you.

—Justin Gonzalez

The collaborative team members would also like to give special thanks to Meg Ormiston, who saw a spark in them and then encouraged them to pass it on and share their love for teaching with others.

Acknowledgments

Solution Tree Press would like to thank the following reviewers:

Shalonda Carr
Fourth- and Fifth-Grade ESL Teacher
Martin Luther King, Jr. Elementary School
Urbana, Illinois

Jodi Hebert
Fourth-Grade Teacher
Eaton Elementary School
Wilmington, North Carolina

Heather Holmes
Technology and STEM Teacher
Advent Episcopal School
Birmingham, Alabama

Xanthy Karamanos
Fourth-Grade Teacher
Benjamin Franklin Elementary School
Edison, New Jersey

Sean Maloney
Fourth-Grade Teacher
Brooklyn Elementary School
Brooklyn, Connecticut

Beth Parker-Van Den Hoek
Fifth- and Sixth-Grade Teacher
Easton School
Easton, Washington

Heather Reit
Digital Integration Specialist
Leaphart Elementary School
Columbia, South Carolina

Kimberly Rouse
Technology Resource Teacher
Newton-Lee Elementary School
Ashburn, Virginia

Visit **go.SolutionTree.com/technology** to download the free reproducibles in this book.

Table of Contents

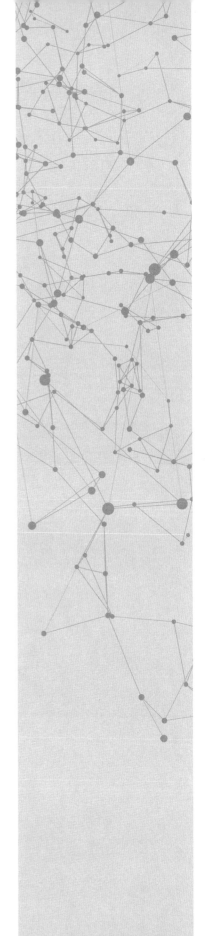

About the Authors

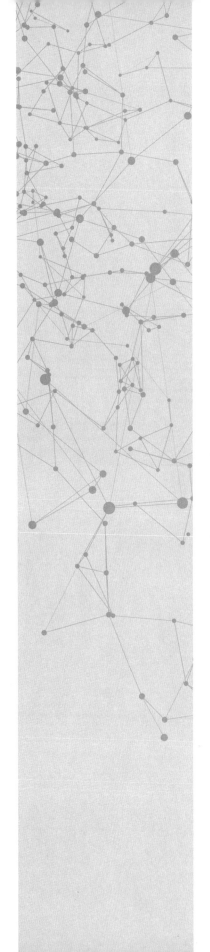

Meg Ormiston is on a mission to change the world of education. She shares her passion for teaching and learning with technology through her keynote speaking, through her writing, and on social media. Meg was a classroom teacher for twelve years and now travels nationally and internationally, speaking about the power of teaching and learning with digital tools. When Meg is home in the Chicago suburbs, you will often find her in classrooms serving as an instructional coach.

In her role as a consultant, Meg partners with school systems that are committed to 21st century learning experiences for everyone. Meg creates a unique partnership in each district, reflecting the mission, vision, and direction that local leaders have identified. Her districtwide projects have included guiding teams through the visioning process, designing and delivering professional development, facilitating classroom modeling, developing student leaders in technology, and educating parents.

As a thought leader in education technology, Meg has published seven books and is collaborating with a team for the five books in the *NOW Classrooms* series. Meg holds a master's degree in curriculum and instruction from National Louis University.

To learn more about Meg's work, follow @megormi on Twitter.

Sheri DeCarlo, a National Board–certified teacher, is a learning and instructional technology coach at a 1:1 Chromebook intermediate-level school in suburban Chicago. Sheri spent ten years as a classroom teacher before transitioning to technology leadership in various roles as a technology teacher, coordinator, and coach since the 1990s. As a member of her district's technology leadership team, she has provided professional development for district staff and teachers and instructed numerous master's-level technology classes for the district's on-site university program. Sheri has had the honor of presenting at local, state, and national conferences.

Sheri earned her bachelor's degree in elementary education from Northern Illinois University and her master's degree in curriculum and instruction from the University of Illinois at Urbana-Champaign with a concentration in instructional technology. She is pursuing her certification to become a certified education technology leader. She enjoys spending her free time cooking, traveling, and having family movie nights with her husband and two daughters, as well as attending car shows and cruise nights.

To learn more about Sheri's work, follow @d60MaerckerTech on Twitter.

Sonya Raymond has presented to school staff, parents, the Illinois Board of Education, and Illinois state lawmakers, and at an Illinois Computing Educators mini-conference in the area of technology. Sonya has had a wide variety of teaching experiences in third grade through eighth grade in multiple U.S. states. Sonya's love of learning has kept her current, and her love for students has kept her passion for teaching alive. Sonya embraces change; she modeled a growth mindset before educators were talking about it.

Sonya attended Southeastern Louisiana University, where she received her bachelor of arts degree, and University of St. Francis, where she received her master's degree in teaching and learning in differentiation. She also received her Type 75 Illinois Administrative Certificate from Concordia University Chicago.

To learn more about Sonya's work, follow @Sonray10 on Twitter.

 **Grace Kowalski** is a master at teaching and learning in the classroom, engaging her young students by using digital tools. She was an elementary teacher in a 1:1 Apple Distinguished School district in suburban Chicago with experience instructing with both tablets and laptops. Grace is now an instructional coach in a K–8 district.

Grace was named an Apple Teacher in 2016, and she is a Google-certified educator. She has presented at local, state, and national conferences and enjoys leading professional development for all teachers.

Grace attended the University of Missouri, where she received her bachelor's degree in elementary education and her master's degree in instruction and curriculum. She is pursuing a master's degree in educational leadership from Concordia University Chicago. Grace is passionate about personalized learning and providing a hands-on, engaging experience for all students.

To learn more about Grace's work, follow @TeamKowalski on Twitter.

 **Justin Gonzalez** is a young, passionate, and innovative educator who believes in the power of education technology. He has experience teaching both first grade and third grade and works in a third-grade inclusion classroom where he co-teaches with a special education teacher to meet the varied needs of students with mild to moderate disabilities. Justin embraces the use of iPads in a 1:1 Apple Distinguished Program and has found many ways to use technology to differentiate for students, enhance learning, and better assess student knowledge

and understanding. He has presented at local and state conferences. At his school, he leads the student-run tech club.

Justin received his bachelor's degree from the University of Illinois at Urbana-Champaign and is pursuing a master's degree in educational leadership from Concordia University Chicago.

To learn more about Justin's work, follow @Mr_JGonzalez on Twitter.

To book Meg Ormiston, Sheri DeCarlo, Sonya Raymond, Grace Kowalski, or Justin Gonzalez for professional development, contact pd@SolutionTree.com.

Introduction

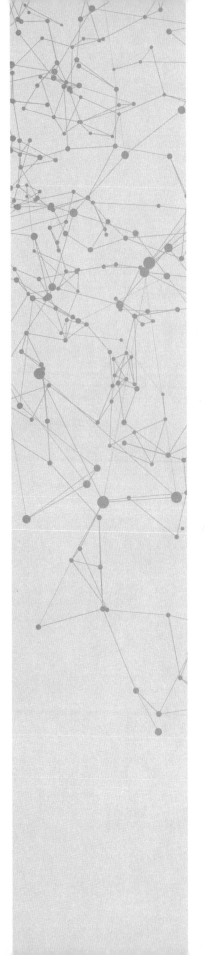

We want to work in schools filled with magical teacher-student partnership classrooms. In these classrooms, students own their data, and they set individual and group goals based on the projects they are working on. Looking around these classrooms, you see what we call *messy learning* or *organized chaos*. Think of the vibe of a busy coffeehouse, everyone chatting or working independently, depending on each person's goals. Digital devices are everywhere, but so are collaboration and all types of communication as everyone gathers for different goals.

Like in a coffeehouse, when you walk into a magical classroom, you feel the energy as all students are laser focused on their personal learning targets and as they collaborate with each other. The teacher has set high expectations for each student, and he or she continuously monitors data using a variety of technology interfaces. Parents and other professionals are part of the communication loop with access to goal-focused data, using a variety of technologies. We call these magical classrooms *NOW classrooms*. We selected that term because our students deserve to thrive in rich learner-centered classrooms *now*, not in a few months or years. We believe schools are ready to create this type of NOW classroom, typified by technology-supported teaching and learning, and the evidence we've seen bears this belief out. Our goal with this book and this series is to help you create them.

While every student in NOW classrooms has individual goals, expectations, and deadlines, the students also engage in extensive collaborative problem solving around rich, real-world problems. Group members and the teacher monitor these projects by using digital tools and face-to-face meetings. For every group project, teachers expect students to connect to an authentic audience beyond the classroom walls to engage subject-area experts and present their findings to others. These presentations might take place in face-to-face settings, but often, the authentic audience comes into the classroom using different technology tools, and the teacher partners with each student to help him or her make connections to outside experts and an authentic audience.

In NOW classrooms, students own their learning. Every student can explain his or her individual learning progression and team progress to any administrator or classroom visitor. Students support what they say with the data they have at their fingertips, using digital devices and different technology interfaces. Students continue to work on their individual and group goals outside of school, where digital tools make collaboration and communication possible. The students know the teacher expects them to demonstrate what they know and can do as a result of what they have learned, and to deliver creative presentations. They might use digital tools to support and deliver their work, but the teacher encourages them to use voice and choice to creatively express themselves.

The teacher is the master conductor in these classrooms, constantly connecting the dots to support and stretch student learning. The role of the teacher in these classrooms has completely shifted from that of classroom content expert to master critical thinker. The students are the active learners and problem solvers, developing these critical skills they will need for their future careers outside of school in offices that potentially look and feel more like the coffeehouse than a building comprising isolated workspaces.

This book provides collections of lessons that support teachers as they encourage students to collaborate in these ways and develop super skills, focus on goals, and make connections beyond the classroom, all of which help you make your classroom magical.

Developing Super Skills Now!

Super skills include the four Cs of communication, collaboration, critical thinking, and creativity (Partnership for 21st Century Skills, 2011). These are not just soft skills but essential skills students need to be successful, lifelong learners in the 21st century. Preparing students for the future is the fundamental reason for formal education, and our students need the four Cs more than they ever have. Every student deserves to become ready for the future as he or she learns how to learn in an ever-changing landscape. With this in mind, we have based the lessons in this book on a foundation of students applying these skills.

We need to develop these super skills in students because in many classrooms, students have not experienced student voice and choice, meaning they have not been allowed to decide how they present the information they learn. By giving students the opportunity for voice and choice in the content, process, and product of their learning, students will develop communication, collaboration, critical thinking, and creativity skills that are specific to their learning styles. NOW classrooms look very different from traditional classrooms because students own their learning path and goals in NOW classrooms. Students become independent directors of their own lifelong learning as they cultivate and apply these skills, ensuring their success outside the classroom.

Focusing on Goals, Not Technology

We know the future is all about change for our students, and we wrote this book for that reason. Collectively as authors, we have seen the good, bad, and ugly when schools roll out technology. When schools issue new technology rollouts without professional development, it leaves teachers to figure out how to transform lessons using the new devices. In these schools, some teachers and students experience success with technology, while little changes in other classrooms across the hall.

We take a different approach to technology in the classroom. We focus on the goals for teaching and learning, and then we look at whether and how we can use technology. Most technology rollouts in schools take the opposite approach by focusing on websites and apps rather than the learning goals. Teachers use the technology tools, but they do not make a connection to a learning outcome or the four Cs. In this model, using technology becomes an event rather than part of the fabric of learning.

You may ask, "What does true technology engagement look like?" This book answers that question by demonstrating the opposite of technology misuse. It features students using technology to create, collaborate, explore, investigate, and share their creations beyond classroom walls. This book structures higher-level thinking and problem solving into every lesson. It includes meaningful lessons with purposeful technology uses that directly tie into International Society for Technology in Education (ISTE) 2016 Standards for Students. ISTE (2016) education technology experts developed the following seven standards for students.

1. **Empowered learner:** Students leverage technology to take an active role in choosing, achieving, and demonstrating competency in their learning goals, informed by the learning sciences.

2. **Digital citizen:** Students recognize the rights, responsibilities, and opportunities of living, learning, and working in an interconnected digital world, and they act and model in ways that are safe, legal, and ethical.

3. **Knowledge constructor:** Students critically curate a variety of resources using digital tools to construct knowledge, produce creative artifacts, and make meaningful learning experiences for themselves and others.

4. **Innovative designer:** Students use a variety of technologies within a design process to identify and solve problems by creating new, useful, or imaginative solutions.

5. **Computational thinker:** Students develop and employ strategies for understanding and solving problems in ways that leverage the power of technological methods to develop and test solutions.

6. **Creative communicator:** Students communicate clearly and express themselves creatively for a variety of purposes using the platforms, tools, styles, formats, and digital media appropriate to their goals.

7. **Global collaborator:** Students use digital tools to broaden their perspectives and enrich their learning by collaborating with others and working effectively in teams locally and globally.

Each chapter in this book provides lessons and instructional practices that support one or more of these standards.

Using This Series

We wrote the *NOW Classrooms* series for teachers and instructional coaches who are ready to focus on teaching and learning first and digital devices second. As we designed the lessons, we included technology devices, including tablets, Chromebooks, and laptops. We also designed the lessons with many opportunities to collaborate around devices if you do not have enough devices for each student to use one (often called a *1:1 classroom*). The series includes the following five titles, all organized around grade-level-appropriate themes adapted from the 2016 ISTE Standards for Students.

1. *NOW Classrooms, Grades K–2: Lessons for Enhancing Teaching and Learning Through Technology*

2. *NOW Classrooms, Grades 3–5: Lessons for Enhancing Teaching and Learning Through Technology*

3. *NOW Classrooms, Grades 6–8: Lessons for Enhancing Teaching and Learning Through Technology*

4. *NOW Classrooms, Grades 9–12: Lessons for Enhancing Teaching and Learning Through Technology*

5. *NOW Classrooms, Leader's Guide: Enhancing Teaching and Learning Through Technology*

Instructional coaches might use all five books in the series for project ideas at all grade levels and for leadership strategies. We have scaffolded the lessons across the series of books so they all flow together. We have organized all the grade-level books in this series in the same way to make it easy for our readers to see how the ideas link together. We believe this series will save you hours of preparation time.

Using This Book

This book features a series of lessons written for grades 3–5 teachers. As teachers, we know how challenging it is to come up with fresh ideas for the classroom each day, so we wrote our lessons in a way that makes getting started simple.

Each of the chapters contains two to four topical sections with three lessons each. Instead of labeling the lessons for grades 3–5, we assigned three levels based on the acronym NOW, which stands for *novice, operational*, and *wow*. Teachers can provide novice lessons to students who are new to the skill or task, operational lessons to students who have had some experience with the skill or task, and wow lessons to students who are ready for an extension. Once we arrived at the three levels, it felt almost like a *Choose Your Own Adventure* book instead of a step-by-step recipe book. Depending on your experience with the technology and your goals for your students, you might jump around to the different sections or move linearly from novice, to operational, to wow. Each lesson has an *I can* statement, written in student-friendly language, to identify the learning goal, and a list of steps to follow for the lesson. We feel that the *I can* statements are important to help the students take ownership of the learning goals. Throughout the book, we also include teaching tips and tech tips to help simplify teachers' use of technology with students and save planning time, and connections to support students and teachers.

Chapter 1, "Embracing Creativity," shows educators how they can support students' voice and choice by giving students options for creating multimedia. These skills will allow students to demonstrate what they know via various types of media. Students start creating and collaborating as they snap digital pictures, create videos, and work with audio. In this selfie-crazed world, we know our students can use audio, take pictures, and create videos on their devices, but now, we will connect those skills to the curriculum.

In chapter 2, "Communicating and Collaborating," educators give students opportunities to practice the four Cs of communication, collaboration, critical thinking, and creativity as they begin to share their work beyond the walls of the classroom. Starting with connecting with peers in the classroom, students will practice providing quality feedback. In this chapter, we introduce social media and how to use it in the classroom. Next, students will collaborate on projects with other students in the building, and finally, students will participate with a global audience through social media.

In chapter 3, "Conducting Research and Curating Information," educators teach students how to identify and use quality online sources. Even though our students have had access to the Internet most of their lives, it doesn't mean they know how to weed out the digital clutter for valid sources. The lessons in this chapter are essential to research at any grade level.

In chapter 4, "Thinking Critically to Solve Problems," educators give students strategies for organizing different tasks and solving problems along with online collaborative tools to help with project workflow. Students will learn how to communicate with peers and others beyond the walls of the classroom using a variety of digital tools and online services.

The focus of chapter 5, "Being Responsible Digital Citizens," is critical to students' future success. As educators, we need to help students understand their digital footprint and what that means to their future success. A positive digital footprint carries importance, and middle-grade students need to know that what goes on the Internet stays on the Internet. As educators, we should guide young learners to make good choices every day in class and even better choices online. We tackle some tough topics in this chapter, including online safety, cyberbullying, and positive digital citizenship.

Chapter 6, "Expanding Technology and Coding Concepts," provides lessons through which students will learn all about cloud computing and file management on devices. Because these practices are changing so fast, we need to ensure our middle-grade students understand cloud computing and how to protect their information. This chapter will provide a foundation of technology concepts and operations to help students gain the skills they need and will need in the future to perform basic technology functions, troubleshoot, and keep their data safe and organized.

We include practical classroom management tips in every chapter in clear, nontechnical language. Each chapter includes discussion questions you can use during personal reflection or when you learn with your colleagues. We also include a comprehensive appendix of terms and tools, featuring many apps, websites, or technology we write about that might help the reader and many other resources that inspired our research. Visit **go.SolutionTree.com/technology** to download a free reproducible version of this appendix. As authors, we understand that not every classroom is uniform, so we provided as many alternatives for resources as possible. We will continue to grow with you and share what we learn on our blog.

Building Background: Know Before You Go

Readers should be aware of a few additional concepts regarding this content before they begin engaging with the lessons and chapters that follow. We want to briefly mention suggestions for the sequence in which readers use the lessons in the book, explain the Google Drive platform to ensure all readers have background knowledge on its tools, discuss the concept of learning management systems, which we mention frequently and which play an important role in many lessons, and emphasize the importance of following policies regarding student privacy and Internet use.

Sequence of Use

We know everyone starts at a different point, so we encourage you to jump around in the book. For example, teachers who struggle with technology integration may want to focus first on chapters 1 and 6. We have filled each chapter with practical lessons you can use in any sequence based on your students' needs. In the appendix, we have included a comprehensive list of every website, app, and product we mention in the book. As digital terms and tools come up, consult definitions in the comprehensive list in the appendix. Visit

go.SolutionTree.com/technology to access live links to the sites mentioned in this book.

Learning Management Systems

Schools in the 21st century use many different software programs and web-based applications, or *learning management systems* (LMSs). Most learning management systems have some free features and premium school or district solutions. In most schools, everyone uses the same system so students and parents don't need to learn a different LMS for every class. Most learning management systems allow the teacher to message students, assign and collect documents, report student progress, and deliver e-learning content. Throughout the book, you will notice we provide steps for how the teacher gives digital files to students and then how students return the digital files to the teacher through the class LMS. For example, "Have students copy the URL and submit the link on the class LMS" means students copy the web address from their document or product they created and share it through the class LMS.

Common learning management systems, both free and fee based, include the following, but you can find hundreds of others on the market.

- Schoology (www.schoology.com)
- Canvas (www.canvaslms.com)
- Edmodo (www.edmodo.com)
- Otus (https://otus.com)
- PowerSchool Learning (www.powerschool.com /solutions/lms)
- Blackboard (www.blackboard.com)
- Moodle (https://moodle.org)
- D2L (www.d2l.com)
- Pearson SuccessNet (www.pearsonsuccessnet.com)

Most districts will select a learning management system for consistency across the district. One free option that needs a little more explanation is Google Classroom (https://classroom .google.com). Google Classroom is a cross between a document management system and a learning management system. It does not contain all the features of an LMS, but it is a great way to get started with managing a digital classroom. Imagine a whole new world without a stack of papers to grade in which every assignment submitted gets organized and recorded in digital folders. Start your LMS search with your trusted colleagues, and soon, you will manage your class digitally.

We can't imagine teaching without an LMS. If the LMS changed for whatever reason, we would easily adapt to the new features of the next system, but we can't imagine ever going back to a paper-based system. With a paper system, it is easier to misfile documents, it is harder to communicate with other collaborators, and it makes it more difficult for students to collaborate with one another. Please reach out to your technology department for specific help, or we are always happy to support your personal professional development when you connect with us on Twitter.

Student Privacy and Internet Use Policies

In many of the lessons, you will see students share their work beyond classroom walls. This connection to the outside world is an important one. As educators, we make it our goal to prepare students for the world beyond the classroom, and they live in a connected world. We mention publishing student work online throughout the book, but before you start tweeting pictures or sharing student work online, make sure you understand your school's and district's policies for sharing information on social media. Talk to your administrator, and ensure that you understand what you can and can't share online. In addition to staying mindful of school and district policy, you should familiarize yourself with the Children's Online Privacy Protection Act of 1998 before you have students publicly share their work.

Assessment

Designing effective assessments for student-created digital projects is a process of providing specific feedback throughout the creation process, not just at the end with a letter grade. This team of authors has discovered that short formative assessment checkpoints as students are collaborating and creating projects is the best way to help students better understand the curriculum as well as the technology tools. Feedback might come from the teacher, another student, or another classroom across the globe.

This author team believes in creative assessments that include planning before the project about what will be assessed based on the learning outcome. Regardless of the technology tool, app, or website, the assessment feedback must stay laser focused on the specific *I can* statements in each lesson. For example, the assessment feedback should not be about how many transitions are in a PowerPoint presentation. Instead, the feedback should be focused on the mastery of the content connected to the learning objective. Creating digital student projects, artifacts, and examples is part of almost every lesson in the book, with each project demonstrating a mastery of content.

We encourage students to organize the projects they create during the year in a digital portfolio. A simple way to get started is by using a Google Doc. Students can create a hyperdoc, in other words, one document with hyperlinks out to the digital projects they have created. This hyperdoc becomes the evidence of completion and growth over time. Another way students participate in the assessment process is when they build their digital portfolio on a website like Seesaw (http://web.seesaw.me). A more advanced digital portfolio could be created using the free Google Sites, a simple-to-create, template-driven website that can be shared publically.

Conclusion

We want to put in your hands great ways to use technology across a curriculum. We have written about how we avoid technology abuse in our classrooms. We offer lessons structured around communication, collaboration, critical thinking, and creativity, with higher-level thinking and problem solving connected to the learning outcome for every lesson.

We made it our goal to create a practical, reader-friendly book, blog, Twitter hashtag, and website (http://nowclassrooms.com) for the teacher using technology in the classroom. We created our own personal learning network (PLN) as we collaborated on this book, helping each other keep the focus

UNDERSTANDING HASHTAGS

Hashtags can organize groups around topics of interest. They begin with what you may know as a *pound sign*. For example, our writing team's hashtag is #NOWClassrooms. We know that the tools and apps will change, so we will provide updates to our readers using our blog and website using the #NOWClassrooms hashtag. If you want to keep up with our research and activities, you should follow the hashtag on Facebook and Twitter.

CONNECT WITH US ON TWITTER

Meg Ormiston:
@megormi

Sheri DeCarlo:
@d60MaerckerTech and @sdecarlo20

Sonya Raymond:
@sonray10

Grace Kowalski:
@TeamKowalski

Justin Gonzalez:
@Mr_JGonzalez

on teaching and learning first and then matching the right technology to the goals. Visit our blog at http://nowclassrooms.com/blog, where we will provide images of student work and continue to add new project ideas, or join our PLN on Twitter at #NOWClassrooms, where we will also post these. We invite you to take a moment to use the hashtag *#NOWClassrooms* to post about your experiences implementing lessons from this book in your classroom. We love to see and hear what classrooms around the world are doing!

We don't know specifically what jobs we are preparing our students for, but we know they need the four Cs we have woven throughout the book. We are excited to see the projects your students create, and your success is our success. Have fun on your journey!

Embracing Creativity

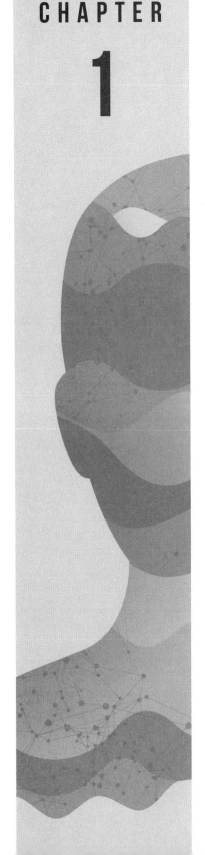

Preparing students for jobs that have not yet been created, let alone thought about, stands as a monstrous task for any educator. ISTE (2016) Standards for Students encourage all learners to be creative communicators, innovative designers, and computational thinkers. Throughout this chapter, these standards guide the lessons to assist students to create and publish projects in a variety of different ways. This involves creating a classroom in which problem solving and critical thinking remain at the forefront. Throughout the book, you will hear us talk about student voice and choice that allows student decision making throughout the creative process.

Lessons in this chapter focus on deepening students' creativity and innovation skills through a range of tasks—from simply recording their voices to developing skills in multimedia creation, regardless of device. According to Michael Hernandez (2015):

> Multimedia stories are fun challenges for your students and empower them to share their ideas and concerns with the wider world. We owe them the opportunity to become multimedia literate and to develop the courage it takes to have an impact on society.

This chapter will provide teachers with tools to give students the power to create their ideas for others to see. We share lessons that combine student interest and creativity that will engage and excite teachers and students alike. The lessons in this chapter cover the tasks of working with digital images, creating video projects, working with audio, and creating meaningful multimedia projects. For information about the tools we mention in these lessons, and for clarity on technology terms you may encounter in this chapter, see the appendix on page 133. Visit **go.SolutionTree.com/technology** to download a free reproducible version of this appendix and to access live links to the tools mentioned in this book.

Working With Digital Images

Teachers will have students work individually and in small groups to create projects using digital images to demonstrate what they have learned. Students will then share projects with an authentic audience beyond the walls of the classroom. Working with images is a nonlinguistic representation that often leads to deeper understanding of a topic. So much of the work we do in schools is focused on developing language skills, but it is important that students also learn how to create a message using images. Students will learn that they can use digital images to better understand concepts and ideas and demonstrate what they have learned.

Novice: Searching for Digital Images

This lesson covers searching for digital images, saving them, and using the images in a project. Students will use voice and choice to select the best resource to create a project. The purpose of searching for digital images, saving them, and using the images in a chosen project is to provide students with an authentic opportunity to share their voice through digitally enhanced projects. Students can use these skills in all types of multimedia projects in all content areas. We encourage students to collaborate in groups as they learn a new app, website, or program.

Process: Searching Online for Images

To complete the following six lesson steps, we recommend you use a search engine; our favorite is Google (www.google .com). If you prefer, you can adapt this process for use with a variety of other options including Microsoft Bing (www.bing .com) or Yahoo! (www.yahoo.com). In the tech tips, we have included other student-friendly search engines.

Learning goal:

I can search for digital images, save them, and use the images in a project.

Use a search engine to complete the following six steps for this lesson.

1. Tell students to open the search engine and search for a curriculum-related topic.

2. From the results screen, have them select Images to display only images.

3. Students can narrow the search if needed using more specific terms or filter features, and then they can select an image.

4. Tell students they should not save by right-clicking the image from this screen. This could result in a low-resolution image that may look pixelated or fuzzy when placed in a project. Instead, they should first click on the image so that it expands to fill most of the screen.

5. Once students click through to the larger image, they should right-click on and save this high-resolution image. On a tablet, students should hold their finger on the image and save it.

6. To address copyright issues, students should also copy the image's web address and paste that link into a document for recording project resources.

Connections

You can apply this lesson to different content areas in the following suggested ways.

- **English language arts:** Groups of students can create a retelling of a picture book from a different point of view. The students make the ebook with digital images they have found online.

- **Mathematics:** Groups of students can search for pictures of real-life examples of three-dimensional shapes.

- **Social science:** Students can search for a primary-source document, saved as an image, and insert this image into a project. These examples can be used in a final project.

- **Science:** Students can search for images online to illustrate a science topic.

TECH TIPS

Students can use the following additional search engines.

▸ **KidRex:** www.kidrex.org

▸ **Safe Search Kids:** www.safesearchkids.com

▸ **Kiddle:** www.kiddle.com

▸ **DinoSearch:** www.dinosearch.com

▸ **Flickr:** www.flickr.com

Following are instructions for saving images on different devices.

▸ **iPad:** Press and hold on the image > select Save Image. (The image will save to the Camera Roll.)

▸ **Any tablet:** Press and hold on the image > select Save Image. (The image will save to the Downloads folder.)

▸ **MacBook:** Right-click (or Control + click) on the image > select Save Image As > pick a location to save the image to.

▸ **PC:** Right-click on the image > select Save Image As > pick a location to save the image to.

▸ **Chromebook:** Right-click (or use Alt + one tap on the touch pad) on the image > select Save Image As > select Choose My Drive. (Note that the location defaults to Downloads, which can be very difficult to retrieve.)

▸ **Universal keystroke shortcut:** Hold down Control or Command + S.

- **Art:** Students can search for, save, and insert into a presentation different images from one artist.

- **Physical education:** Students can search for images specific to a sport or activity they do in class. They can play the slideshow of images on a screen outside the school gym so other students in the school can see them.

Operational: Annotating Digital Photos

The purpose of this lesson is to have students demonstrate their thinking by annotating an image using a variety of technology tools. Students use higher-level thinking in this type of multimedia creation, or mashing up of media, as they add details and information to an existing image. Students will focus on adding text, labels, or other elements to a base image to show deeper thinking or understanding of the content.

Process: Using Diagramming Software to Annotate a Digital Image

To complete the following six lesson steps, we recommend you use Google Drawings (https://drawings.google.com). If you prefer, you can adapt this process for use with a variety of other options. Options include but are not limited to Microsoft Paint, PicCollage (https://pic-collage.com), and the native photo app on the device.

1. Have students locate a base image before beginning annotations. For example, in science, students would need to search for an image of a cell as the base image before they can label the parts of the cell.

2. Students should open Google Drawings, found in their Google Drive, and search for a base image to annotate.

3. Have students add text boxes on top of the image to show what they have learned about the topic.

4. As the teacher, you may set how many annotations students need to include based on the content you cover.

5. In addition to text boxes, students can also add other features like lines and shapes.

TEACHING TIPS

▸ Many students have experience annotating pictures on social media, but the key to this lesson is to see what students have learned based on your instruction or their research.

▸ Students annotating an image helps the teacher understand the students' thought processes as they are creating a project.

6. When students finish, they can share their drawing just like any other Google Drive document using the class LMS.

Connections

You can apply this lesson to different content areas in the following suggested ways.

- **English language arts:** Students can search for an image and annotate the image to show how it relates to or reflects aspects of a piece of writing.

- **Mathematics:** Students can take a photo of a problem they solved on paper and use the annotation features to explain how they solved the problem. Also, students can annotate or label the properties of any geometric shape (sides, angles, symmetry, and so on) on an image of the shape to demonstrate the learning target that the teacher has created.

- **Social science:** Students can select a primary-source image and annotate the image to demonstrate what they learned about the topic. You could collect these student-created examples in a Google Slides presentation, creating a multimedia study guide.

- **Science:** Students can take a photo of an experiment and annotate their findings. Students and teachers can work together to decide when this would be most useful to their learning objective.

- **Art:** Students can take a picture of something they have created and annotate the image to share what they learned about the specific style of art.

Wow: Enhancing Digital Photos

The purpose of this lesson is to provide students with a creative outlet to demonstrate their learning through enhancing digital photos. This higher-level technology skill has students critically study the base image they select and enhance it to demonstrate what they have learned. For example, in English language arts, students find an image to use with their piece of writing, but they determine the image would better match the tone of the piece if it appeared in black and white. With these new skills, students can modify an image to make it

---

TECH TIPS

▸ Different applications and websites have different annotation features, including labels and drawings; sizing options; the ability to rotate, flip, or move items; and so on.

▸ When students save their final image, the annotations are embedded with the original image, creating one easy-to-share image.

Learning goal:
I can edit and manipulate a photo to enhance its purpose.

black and white. Students can apply these photo-editing skills to more sophisticated presentations in the future.

Process: Editing Photos Online With Photo-Editing Software

To complete the following four lesson steps, we recommend you use PicMonkey (www.picmonkey.com), a free online image editor. If you prefer, you can adapt this process for use with a variety of other options. Other options may offer different features. For example, Photoshop (www.adobe.com/photoshop) is used for modifying and enhancing images, whereas PicCollage (https://pic-collage.com) can be used to add multiple photos into one final collage. We encourage teachers to allow students to choose the application that works best for their project, device, and learning style.

1. Students should take a picture with their device. The image is saved with other photos on the device or uploaded to the student's Google Drive.

2. Have students navigate to the website PicMonkey (www.picmonkey.com), using a web browser. Students should select an image from their device that they would like to enhance. Once the image is selected, students should upload the image to the PicMonkey website and select the pencil icon in the upper-right corner.

3. Students can crop the image and change the light, color, and more.

4. Have students save and share the newly modified image.

Connections

You can apply this lesson to different content areas in the following suggested ways.

- **Cross-curricular teaching:** Students can search for multiple pictures to tell a story or give step-by-step instructions of a process. By editing or manipulating these photos, students can clearly demonstrate what they are learning.

- **English language arts:** Using story elements, students can order pictures and enhance and annotate them to create a comic to retell a story

---

TECH TIPS

▸ Photo manipulation options include adding labels, text, drawings, and shapes; changing sizes; and rotating, flipping, and moving images. Each of the different photo-editing apps has different features. For example, Photoshop has the most advanced features for professional use. Many of the other sites have simpler features and are easier for students to use.

▸ Photo-editing options include cropping, adding filters, changing contrast and brightness, and more.

the class has read or to create an original story. For nonfiction texts, students can add captions or label photos to identify the steps in a process to complete a task.

- **Social science:** Students can search for an image from history and modernize it using digital tools. Students can Photoshop themselves into a primary-source image.

- **Science:** Students can search for photos or use their own photos of an experiment or a scientific principle they study. Students can save, categorize, and order images in a project according to sequence, progression, or complexity. They can annotate or label claims and evidence of the principle taught, such as matter phase changes, weather fronts, and the plant life cycle.

- **Art:** Students can take a picture of their original artwork and digitally modify the piece. They can then compare and contrast the two images.

Creating Video Projects

Creating videos is one way students demonstrate what they have learned. There are many free and low-cost options for creating videos on different types of devices. Depending on the devices your students will use to create the videos, we have included a variety of websites, apps, and programs. We've included a range of tools because not all classrooms will have access to the same platforms. For example, the program iMovie (www.apple.com/imovie) is only available for Macs, and the app is available for iPhones and iPads. Throughout the lessons on creating video projects, we emphasize that planning is important. Tony Vincent's blog, *Learning in Hand*, includes valuable resources to help students prepare and think through video projects. The post "Plan a Better iMovie Trailer With These PDFs" (Vincent, 2014; http://bit.ly /1yjjSMX) shares storyboard templates students can use with iMovies as they plan for creating a video. If you are using a different video platform, feel free to create a template for your students, or have students use paper and pencil.

Learning goal:

I can create a book trailer and share it outside my classroom.

Novice: Creating Book Trailers

The purpose of this lesson is for students to create a trailer for a book they have read to summarize their understanding of the targeted learning goal. The trailer should hook their audience without giving away too many of the book's details. Students should make sure they understand the trailer's purpose before they start filming and planning. Students can find many examples of book and movie trailers on YouTube (www.youtube.com).

Process: Using Video-Editing Software to Create Book Trailers

To complete the following five lesson steps, we recommend you use an iPad or Mac, as they both come with iMovie (www.apple.com/imovie) preinstalled. If you prefer, you can use this process with a variety of other options such as Magisto (www.magisto.com) and Animoto (https://animoto .com). With many options available, teachers should allow the students to choose the application that best fits their needs and the devices they have available.

1. Have groups of students open iMovie on a Mac or iPad and select Trailer.

2. The groups should select the template they would like to use. Exploring and selecting templates in iMovie takes time for groups of students.

3. After choosing their trailer, students will access the planning document at http://bit.ly/1yjjSMX to plan their iMovie.

4. Once the planning document is complete, students should sequence the photos or videos they use and add titles and transitions.

5. When the students finish, have them share their final published trailer.

Connections

You can apply this lesson to different content areas in the following suggested ways.

- **Cross-curricular teaching:** Students can create movie trailers as a study guide around a unit.

- **English language arts:** Students can create a review of a book, chapter, or section they have read by creating a book trailer.

- **Mathematics:** Students can create a movie trailer about what they have learned in a mathematics unit of study that you can use as a summative assessment.

- **Social science:** Students can create a *Choose Your Own Adventure* type of movie trailer to show how a historical event could have changed had different decisions been made.

- **Science:** Students can take digital pictures as they work through a lab experiment and create a movie trailer about the process.

- **Physical education:** Students can create a movie trailer about a sport or activity.

Operational: Creating Multimedia Projects With Photos or Video

The purpose of this lesson is to let students have voice and choice as they create multimedia projects connected to curricular goals. The use of photos or video in a multimedia project allows students to visually demonstrate their understanding of a particular standard or topic.

Process: Using Adobe Spark to Create Multimedia

To complete the following three lesson steps, we recommend you use Adobe Spark (https://spark.adobe.com), a free website to design graphics, images, videos, and webpages. The templates it contains make it easy for teachers and students to create projects. If you prefer, you can adapt this process for use with a variety of other options. Other options include but are not limited to WeVideo (www.wevideo.com), Google Sites (https://sites.google.com), Google Slides (www.google.com/slides/about), and PowerPoint.

1. Prior to students creating a multimedia project, they should decide what their message is and how to best share that message. Students should compile a variety of photos or videos that they would like to include in the project.

2. Students will navigate to http://spark.adobe.com and log in using their Google accounts. Once logged in, students can either create a post, page, or video to demonstrate their learning. Adobe Spark provides step-by-step instructions for each option as well as very helpful video introductions.

3. Have students share what they have created using the class LMS.

Connections

You can apply this lesson to different content areas in the following suggested ways.

- **English language arts:** Students can choose to use photos or video to create a character study of a fictional character.

- **Mathematics:** Groups of students can create multimedia projects to demonstrate how they solved a complex problem.

- **Social science:** Groups of students can create multimedia projects re-enacting a historical event.

- **Science:** Students can demonstrate multiple strategies or scientific principles using photos or video.

- **Physical education:** Students can work in partners to create videos about the proper way to throw a baseball, dribble a basketball, or serve a volleyball.

- **Foreign language:** Students can create videos or multimedia projects and narrate them in the language they are studying.

Wow: Mashing Up Video, Photos, and Audio Into a Project

This lesson focuses on giving students an outlet to demonstrate their understanding of what they have learned in a multimedia format. Students may have different file formats, including photos, videos, and audio files, to demonstrate their learning.

Process: Creating Movies

To complete the following four lesson steps, we recommend you use WeVideo (www.wevideo.com), an online video editor with free and premium features. If you prefer, you can adapt this process for use with a variety of other options. Options include but are not limited to TouchCast (www.touchcast .com) and iMovie (www.apple.com/imovie).

1. Students should access WeVideo through their Google Drive by clicking on New > More > Connect More Apps, and then search for WeVideo. They only have to do this once because WeVideo will now be linked to their Google Drive account.

2. Have students upload the images they have already chosen to use in their movie to WeVideo. Keep in mind that some apps or programs require specific file formats for compatibility.

3. Students should sequence the images and add sound effects and music from the collection within WeVideo. By using the sounds and music in WeVideo, teachers will have no concern about students violating copyright in their projects.

4. Once students complete their videos, have the students publish them and share them with an authentic audience beyond the walls of the classroom.

Connections

You can apply this lesson to different content areas in the following suggested ways.

- **English language arts:** Groups of students can create a movie of a different ending to a book they read. Also, they can change a portion of a story and retell it with different settings and characters.

- **Mathematics:** Groups of students can take specific mathematics strategies and find examples in real life, creating a multimedia project of these examples that they can share.

- **Social science:** Groups of students can create a prequel to a historical event in any multimedia

TEACHING TIPS

- ▶ Have students distinguish the difference between a single image and a framed video.

- ▶ You or your students can determine who will see the final movies and what message you want them to get from watching the movies.

- ▶ Allow students to select the technology tools they use in their movies to support student voice and choice.

TECH TIPS

- ▶ Photo and video files can be saved in the following formats.

  - > **Photo:** .jpg, .png, .tif, and .gif

  - > **Video:** .mp4, .mov, .avi, .mpg, and .flv

- ▶ If an image a student wants to use appears in the wrong file format or is corrupt, have the student search for another image with the correct file format. For example, the file format .jpg is the most common for images, but sometimes students will find an image with the file extension .png, .bmp, or .gif. Depending on the app or the program a student is using, the file format of a specific image may not be compatible.

project, explaining cause-and-effect relationships that led to the event.

- **Science:** Groups of students can create movies illustrating what a day without a simple machine would look like. Assign a different simple machine to each group, and have students tell their story with simple machines found around the school.

- **Art:** Students can create a multimedia project using classmates' authentic artwork to show different art styles.

Working With Audio

Creating audio clips can help students discuss what they learned and reflect on their learning. Most devices have an audio-recording app that is native to the device. Using this feature allows the teacher to understand students' thought process, check their fluency, and give oral feedback. Using audio is yet another option for students to choose as they demonstrate their learning.

Novice: Recording My Thinking

Across the curriculum, we often ask our students, "How did you get your answer?" or "Can you explain your thinking?" This lesson focuses on these questions as students record their thought process while working through a problem. When students can listen to themselves as they work through a problem, they can improve their academic vocabulary and catch their mistakes.

Process: Using a Voice-Recording Tool

To complete the following six lesson steps, we recommend you use Fluency Tutor (https://fluency.texthelp.com/Chrome /Get), an extension in Google Chrome. If you prefer, you can adapt this process for use with a variety of other options. Some options include but are not limited to Audacity (www .audacityteam.org) and Educreations (www.educreations .com). However, we chose to focus on Fluency Tutor for this lesson because of the feedback this tool provides. With other options, teachers will listen to the audio clips and provide feedback to the students themselves.

Learning goal:
I can use a variety of tools to record my thoughts and opinions.

1. Students or teachers add Fluency Tutor to their devices by downloading the application before the lesson begins.

2. Create an account to manage the data students collect as they read and record passages.

3. Share a passage of text with the class, and have students read the passage aloud while the Fluency Tutor app records the audio.

4. Students can use the helpful embedded tools, including a picture dictionary and text-to-speech conversion.

5. In Fluency Tutor, use the data dashboard to see class progress and listen to the passages of individual students and color-code the errors.

6. Students can always go back and listen to their own recordings to self-reflect on their fluency in addition to the teacher using these recordings for assessment and feedback.

Connections

You can apply this lesson to different content areas in the following suggested ways.

- **English language arts:** Students can record themselves reading a story and practicing their best reading. Students should listen to the audio and then try to read the same passage out loud again to make their reading more fluent. Students save both audio clips to compare and contrast them.

- **Mathematics:** Students can record an explanation of a mathematics problem. As an extension idea, have students listen to each other's explanations and see if they can solve the problem just by following the steps listed in the recording. Students can then give each other feedback on their mathematics explanations.

- **Social science:** Have students compare and contrast audio recordings created by different students portraying different historical figures from different eras.

TEACHING TIPS

▸ Allow *sandbox time* for students to explore new apps or websites. We use the term *sandbox* to reference playing in a sandbox. We want students to play with and learn the capabilities of an app or website. This prevents the technology from distracting students from the lesson objective.

▸ You can decide whether the students record once or have multiple attempts at recording.

▸ Some students may need to practice before recording, or the teacher may decide that it has to be a cold read. A *cold read* is reading without previously practicing the text.

TECH TIPS

▸ In a loud classroom environment, consider using a microphone or a headset with a microphone to reduce interference when recording audio.

▸ The teacher should determine where the audio files are stored or shared. Some ideas include posting in a Google Form, sharing in a folder, or sending an email or message.

- **Science:** Have groups of students create an audio summary about what they learned from an experiment.

- **Physical education:** Have students record directions or coaching tips for other students to follow.

Operational: Manipulating Multiple Audio Files

This lesson focuses on combining multiple audio files together in order to create a final piece. During certain tasks or projects, students will have multiple audio recordings that they might need to combine in order to demonstrate their learning. Students can adjust the volume on these audio files and put them in a certain order for their final project.

Process: Recording Actions and Audio With an Interactive Whiteboard App

To complete the following four lesson steps, we recommend you use Explain Everything (https://explaineverything.com), an app and a Chrome extension that you can use on almost any device, computer, or tablet that uses the Google Chrome browser. If you prefer, you can adapt this process for use with a variety of other options. Options include but are not limited to the Chrome extension Screencastify (www.screen castify.com) and the website and app Educreations (www .educreations.com).

1. Have students navigate to the app Explain Everything or launch the Explain Everything extension within Chrome on a Chromebook.

2. Students will plan out their presentation and sequence pictures to illustrate the main points.

3. Use the tools within Explain Everything to crop, add voice over, and manage audio clips to create a final project.

4. The app pulls everything together into a movie that students can share through the class LMS.

Learning goal:
I can splice together pieces of audio and adjust the volume as needed.

↑ TEACHING TIPS

▸ Students should practice with a classmate to make the audio-creation process easier.

▸ Make sure that the students stay focused on the learning objective. If necessary, provide scaffolding with a graphic organizer or storyboard that will allow the students to stay focused on the academic skills.

Connections

You can apply this lesson to different content areas in the following suggested ways.

- **English language arts:** Students can create a retelling of an event by making an audio recording and adding sound effects that reflect or enhance the content they are creating. English learners could also change a portion of a story to tell it from a different point of view. This can be used to tell a story from a different cultural perspective or from a different character's point of view, to practice conjugating verbs.

- **Mathematics:** Groups of students can create guess-my-shape narrations in which they explain the attributes that describe the geometric shapes, adding sound effects or music. Students can also record themselves modeling how to solve a mathematics problem in different ways. They then splice together the different pieces of audio to make one recording of the different explanations.

- **Social science:** Students can create a narrative around an event, such as what would have happened if the United States had never landed a man on the moon. Students can tell the story, incorporating different points of view using alternative voices (for example, voices for a newscaster, a cowboy, and an astronaut), and use a lot of expression and inflection to enhance the recording.

- **Science:** Groups of students can create weather report narratives by pretending to be a meteorologist on a radio broadcast or a podcast focusing on climate change.

Wow: Engaging My Audience With Sound Effects

In this lesson, students will enhance their projects by adding sound effects to engage their audience. The use of certain sound effects can enhance a presentation; however, sound effects also can distract the audience. Students need to discover when it seems appropriate to use certain sound effects

TECH TIPS

▸ In a loud classroom environment, consider using a microphone or a headset with a microphone to reduce interference during recording.

▸ With all technology, teachers should try the technology first to ensure that it works properly before students record.

Learning goal:
I can edit and enhance multiple audio clips by adding sound effects to create a final product.

and when it may be appropriate to leave the project without audio distractions.

Process: Enhancing a Project With Sound Effects

To complete the following six lesson steps, we recommend you use VoiceThread (https://voicethread.com) to set up an online collaborative space for students to create video, voice, and text commenting. VoiceThread is a paid subscription service. If you prefer, you can adapt this process for use with a variety of other options. Options include but are not limited to iMovie (www.apple.com/imovie), PowerPoint, Voki (www.voki.com), and WeVideo (www.wevideo.com).

1. Have students navigate to https://voicethread.com and create an account.

2. Students will click the Create button in the top-left hand corner to then add media. A menu will pop up and students click Audio Recording.

3. If it is the first time that students are using the program, they should allow access to the microphone. The program then begins recording immediately.

4. When recording is complete, students click on the red button. They should then give their project a title and description, and save.

5. Students can edit and enhance recording as needed through tools in VoiceThread. Some of these tools include doodling, adding video, and uploading a comment.

6. Students can then add multimedia comments and share presentations.

Connections

You can apply this lesson to different content areas in the following suggested ways.

- **English language arts:** Students make an audio recording as they retell a story, changing one element of the story, such as the location or time period. Students then react to the change in location as if they were the characters in the story in the audio recording. Students can modify the audio clip based on the element they change. For example, if the setting has changed to the top of a mountain, they might add howling wind to the clip.

- **Mathematics:** Students can create audio reports as they identify mathematical concepts outside the classroom, such as doubling a recipe, which would include the mathematical concept of adding fractions. Students should be creative as they create their audio clips, for example by including sound effects like the blender operating or an oven door opening if they are creating a recipe.

- **Social science:** Students can create a report from a historic event, including background sounds.

- **Science:** Students can use multiple audio clips to create a real-world report. For example, students can report on changing weather conditions. Students can then insert sound effects (such as wind, rain, and sirens) into the recording to enhance their final report.

- **Music:** Students can create a new musical composition, using tracks of music from various sources and adding in their own sound effects to enhance the audio track.

Creating Meaningful Multimedia Projects

In these lessons, students will focus on gathering multiple types of resources to create one multimedia project, giving students the ability to have voice and choice as they draw upon visual, audio, and annotation tools to create a multimedia project that demonstrates their learning.

Novice: Using Visuals to Show My Learning

Teachers can check how well students understand a task, lesson, or unit by having them create a visual aid. Prior to the pervasiveness of technology in our lives and classrooms, students used poster board and markers, but now, they can

Learning goal:
I can create a multimedia poster, embedding photos and text to demonstrate my understanding.

show the world what they know using multimedia. This lesson focuses on creating multimedia posters that embed text and photos.

Process: Creating Visuals

To complete the following three lesson steps, we recommend you use Lucidpress (www.lucidpress.com), a website where students and teachers can create stunning brochures, fliers, digital magazines, newsletters, and reports. It does not require users to install anything on a device, and users can add all types of media to their project with a simple drag-and-drop interface. If you prefer, you can adapt this process for use with a variety of other options. Other options include but are not limited to Adobe Spark (https://spark.adobe.com), Google Slides (www.google.com/slides/about), Google Sites (https://sites.google.com), and Canva (www.canva.com).

1. Have students navigate to www.lucidpress.com. From there, students should click Sign Up With Google and enter their Google information.

2. Students then click on Start a New Document. Students create a poster by using the tools along the left-hand side of the screen. They have the option to add text, shapes, images, tables, videos, and buttons to external links. The teacher should allow students to have the autonomy to create a digital poster as they see fit, utilizing a blank poster or a template. Have students select the type of project they would like to create, and tell them to start to add pieces of media.

3. When students complete their projects, they can share them as a printed graphic or online using a hyperlink.

Connections

You can apply this lesson to different content areas in the following suggested ways.

- **English language arts:** As your class studies persuasive writing, have students create multimedia posters to sell ideas they come up with to others.

- **Mathematics:** Have students create multimedia posters that show an understanding of how to solve a two-step problem.

- **Social science:** Have students create multimedia posters about a current event.

- **Science:** Have students create multimedia posters to explain mitosis.

- **Art:** Have students create multimedia posters with their original artwork as the base image and additional details layered over the image so students can identify different characteristics of various styles of art.

Operational: Finding the Best Way to Demonstrate My Learning

This lesson focuses on students creating multimedia presentations that incorporate photos, video, and audio clips to demonstrate their learning. Students will have the freedom to pick what content they want to share in their presentations. Students will gather research and find the best way to demonstrate their learning throughout the duration of the project.

Process: Collaborating On Multimedia Presentations

To complete the following six lesson steps, we recommend you use Google Slides (www.google.com/slides/about), which is part of Google Drive and is available as a website and an app. If you prefer, you can adapt this process for use with a variety of other options. Options include but are not limited to PowerPoint, Keynote (www.apple.com/keynote), and Haiku Deck (www.haikudeck.com).

1. Arrange students into groups. One student per group should navigate to his or her Google Drive, click New, and select Google Slides, and title the presentation.

2. The student who is the owner of the slide show creates at least one new slide for each topic or idea to be shared in the presentation.

Learning goal:
I can create a multimedia presentation utilizing photos, video, or audio to demonstrate my learning.

3. After the initial slides are created, the student should click the Share icon at the top of the screen and invite the remaining group members.

4. All students add content (text, pictures, sounds, or videos) to each slide. Students may divide up the pages and work separately or work simultaneously on each page.

5. Groups of students can collaborate anytime from anywhere on the same presentation using Google Slides.

6. When students finish their presentations, they can share them through the class LMS or by sharing hyperlinks to the presentations via an application such as Seesaw, Google Classroom, or Google Sites.

Connections

You can apply this lesson to different content areas in the following suggested ways.

- **Cross-curricular teaching:** Students can create slides to demonstrate step-by-step solutions. Teachers can use these as a formative assessment to gauge understanding of specific lesson content.

- **English language arts:** Have students create products and create a *Shark Tank*–like presentation that includes the use of a visual aid. In this presentation, students will attempt to persuade their audience. Students can create presentation slides based on their research, integrating photos, video, and audio where needed, and then pitch their ideas to classmates.

- **Mathematics:** Students can work in groups to explain multiple ways to solve the same mathematics problem on slides.

- **Social science:** Groups of students can create multimedia visuals to support their side of a debate.

- **Science:** Have students integrate audio, video, and photos to further explain the real-world application and the reason behind each step, for example, the water cycle, a lab experiment, or a procedure on how to use a Bunsen burner.

- **Physical education:** Students can create a multimedia visual aid for an upcoming community walk to learn the history of the community or a charity walk. Teachers can showcase these projects on a screen mounted outside the school gym entrance and on the school website.

Wow: Annotating My Multimedia Presentation

The purpose of this lesson is to allow students to create a multimedia presentation and annotate the presentation to share their thoughts and ideas. This lesson takes the creation of a presentation one step forward, as students need to share their thoughts and ways of applying certain concepts. This lesson introduces the term *screencasting*. In screencasting, students capture what appears on the screen of the device they use, along with the audio the students record in real time, and save as a video. The apps, software, and websites to create screencasts vary in features, but each one saves the media into a final movie that students can share with anyone online.

Process: Creating a Screencast

To complete the following three lesson steps, we recommend you use Screencastify (www.screencastify.com), an extension of the Chrome browser. If you prefer, you can adapt this process for use with a variety of other options. Other options include but are not limited to Educreations (www.educreations.com), TouchCast (www.touchcast.com), and Screencast-O-Matic (https://screencast-o-matic.com).

1. Prompt students to add the Screencastify extension to Chrome to create screencasts. This extension is found in the Chrome Web Store (www.google.com /chrome/webstore).

2. Once they have installed Screencastify, an icon appears in the upper-right-hand corner of the screen in the Chrome browser. To create a screencast, have students click on the black film strip icon to start recording the application window or the entire screen.

3. Have students start recording their screen and their narration. Screencastify creates the final video that they can share using a hyperlink.

Learning goal:
I can create and annotate a multimedia presentation to share my thoughts on and interpretations of a concept.

 TEACHING TIPS

- Working in partners works well when students learn how to screencast.

- Consider placing a short time limit on the screencasts, or else students will ramble on.

- A content-focused rubric might help students stay focused on the academic task.

 TECH TIPS

- On most free screencasting apps and extensions, students can't go back and edit. If they make a mistake, chances are they will have to start over.

- Microphones are helpful to reduce the background noise in the classroom.

DISCUSSION QUESTIONS

Consider the following questions for personal reflection or in collaborative work with colleagues.

▸ What educational purpose does annotating photos serve? Which annotation tool do you plan on exploring first?

▸ What purpose does creating book trailer videos serve?

▸ What are three ways to connect to the curriculum using audio files?

▸ How would you explain *screencasting* to someone who has never heard that word?

▸ Why is it important for students to create multimedia projects?

▸ What are three things from this chapter you will share with colleagues?

Connections

You can apply this lesson to different content areas in the following suggested ways.

- **Cross-curricular teaching:** Students can create a screencast explaining content from any subject area.

- **English language arts:** Groups of students can create screencasts inferring what happened in a story.

- **Mathematics:** Students can create a screencast with visuals and audio to explain how to solve a word problem.

- **Social science:** Groups of students can each select a part of the preamble to the U.S. Declaration of Independence and create a screencast to recite or add historical information explaining the part they are viewing.

- **Science:** Students can create a screencast about the life cycle of an animal.

Conclusion

The lesson connections and technology tools in this chapter help make multimedia production a real possibility in all classrooms while supporting students' communication, collaboration, critical thinking, and creativity. Familiarity with using digital images, audio, and video fosters critical skills students need to work with different file formats and content sources and ultimately create multimedia presentations.

All these projects will let students' creativity shine. Soon, you might have a classroom of budding YouTubers, podcasters, and photographers. These powerful skills will help students design and create quality projects they proudly share. The NOW classroom has the potential to differentiate itself from traditional classrooms not because of devices but because teachers allow student voice and choice so students can create for an authentic audience beyond the walls of the classroom. You can use the lessons in this chapter in all content areas as students create in new ways.

Communicating and Collaborating

The 21st century classroom necessitates teachers go beyond the walls of their classrooms, beyond books and paper, and beyond traditional projects. In this chapter, students will connect with an authentic audience as they collaborate and communicate what they have learned in all content areas using different types of technology. The goal of communication and collaboration directly aligns with the creative communicator and global collaborator ISTE (2016) Standards for Students. The lessons in this chapter will help you ensure students practice communication, collaboration, creativity, and critical-thinking skills every day in every content area. Our students need these super skills as they look ahead to future jobs where they will potentially interact with global coworkers.

Connecting to peers at the intermediate level carries as much importance as ever. According to Jennifer Williams (2015), an educational program developer for Edutopia, "Educators can design collaborative learning spaces that will support the teaching and learning of skills needed for the interconnected world of today and tomorrow." The valuable resource of social media, having replaced the landline telephones of the past, allows for interconnectedness in the classroom and beyond, as students share their work and access content in these spaces. Additionally, according to Matt Davis (2012) in his article "How Collaborative Learning Leads to Student Success," "Encouraging students to reach out to each other to solve problems and share knowledge not only builds collaboration skills, it leads to deeper learning and understanding." Global connectedness brings a powerful level of learning never before experienced in classrooms, and we've designed our lessons around this collaborative approach.

The use of instructional videos continues to gain popularity as more classrooms use the *flipped learning* concept, in which students watch teacher-created instructional videos outside of class as homework, and when they come to class, they work collaboratively on hands-on projects instead of listening to the teacher lecture. Done right, flipped learning creates a more active classroom of engaged learners versus a class of students passively listening to a lecture.

We begin this chapter with lessons for creating and using instructional videos. These lessons will help students develop an understanding of what constitutes a quality instructional video and will suggest technology tools for students to use to create their own videos. Next, we provide lessons for connecting with a variety of audiences. These lessons focus on the audience for whom students will create media. Last, we include lessons focused on collaborating and giving feedback. Creation and teaching others are often what determine success. By having students create and share their own instructional videos instead of just watching teacher-created videos, they are becoming empowered learners who demonstrate their knowledge in a meaningful way. Students will understand that using digital tools can help them access and understand learning targets as well as share out their media for feedback and collaboration. For information about the tools we mention in these lessons, and for clarity on technology terms you may encounter in this chapter, see the appendix on page 133. Visit **go.SolutionTree.com/technology** to download a free reproducible version of this appendix and to access live links to the tools mentioned in this book.

Creating and Using Instructional Videos

This section offers a variety of lessons on how to create and use instructional videos. By having students create their own instructional videos, not only are they demonstrating their content knowledge to a greater audience but they are also becoming empowered learners who are communicating in a creative way and connecting to the world around them.

Novice: Evaluating Instructional Videos

Developing a student's background in determining what constitutes a quality video is the objective of this lesson. Teachers show an instructional video and then ask for feedback from students about the quality of the video content and message. The skills developed in this lesson will provide students with the foundation to evaluate the effectiveness of a video and determine if the content matches what they learn.

Process: Creating Rubrics

To complete the following seven lesson steps, we recommend your students use ThemeSpark (www.themespark.net), a website for creating rubrics for projects. The site creates rubrics solely from the standards you will be assessing. If you prefer, you can adapt this process for use with a variety of other options. Options include but are not limited to Rubric Maker (http://rubric-maker.com) and Quick Rubric (www.quickrubric.com). However, you or your students can also choose to make rubrics from scratch using tables in a word processing document. If students are looking to include things that are not in the standards available on ThemeSpark, consider using another one of these options.

1. Navigate to ThemeSpark, and create a teacher account.

2. Have students use their Google logins to sign in to ThemeSpark.

3. Tell students to click on the New Rubric button.

4. Students will select the content area they are creating the rubric for to evaluate the effectiveness of a video to support the content they are learning.

5. Students will then be prompted to select their grade and then the topic they will be covering. All of these options will appear in a drop-down menu.

6. A selection of standards will then appear. Students will be able to click the Select button under the

Learning goal:
I can evaluate the quality and purpose of an instructional video.

TEACHING TIPS

▶ The following resources provide high-quality instructional videos. You may want to have students practice using their rubrics on pre-created high-quality videos and make changes to their rubrics as necessary. What do the students notice in the videos about wait time, examples, step-by-step tutorials, visuals, and so on?

> Khan Academy (www.khanacademy.org) is a website filled with instructional videos across all content areas.

> Teaching Channel (www.teachingchannel.org) is an online community that has high-quality videos for teachers.

> WatchKnowLearn (www.watchknowlearn.org) is a growing website of instructional videos.

standard that they are choosing. Some standards can be broken down even further after this selection.

7. After students complete their rubrics, they can share the rubrics through Google Drive or post the direct URL to each rubric PDF on the class LMS.

Connections

You can apply this lesson to different content areas in the following suggested ways.

- **English language arts:** As a class, brainstorm ideas with students about the elements of a quality instructional video. As a class, watch a YouTube video about a topic like onomatopoeia, and discuss the video quality and content.

- **Mathematics:** Have groups of students compare and contrast different instructional videos on a specific topic, like addition with regrouping.

- **Science:** Locate an instructional video about the scientific topic your class studies, such as interdependent relationships in ecosystems, and have students watch the video to analyze the clarity of the message and the overall content of the video. Discuss and analyze the video's objective, examples, clarity of message, and stability.

- **Art:** Select three different videos related to an instructional unit in art's content, and have students compare and contrast them to describe what makes a good instructional video.

Operational: Creating an Instructional Video

The objective of this lesson is to provide students with the opportunity to demonstrate what they have learned about what constitutes a quality video by having them create their own instructional videos. The skills learned from this lesson create students who think critically and can explain the details of what they have learned.

Learning goal:
I can create a video for my teacher that demonstrates my understanding.

Process: Using Interactive Whiteboard Software to Create a Screencast

People often refer to all interactive whiteboards as *SMART Boards* even though many different manufacturers exist, including SMART Technologies (https://home.smarttech.com), Promethean (www.prometheanworld.com), and Mimio (www.mimioconnect.com). A screen-recording feature in the whiteboard's software records everything happening on the interactive whiteboard along with the voice of the teacher or student who works on the whiteboard. All of the interactive whiteboards we have mentioned include this feature. Use a presentation software program of your choice, such as PowerPoint, Google Slides (www.google.com/slides/about), or Keynote (www.apple.com/keynote), and an interactive whiteboard to complete the following five steps for this lesson.

1. Have groups of students create short presentations using PowerPoint, Google Slides, or Keynote. Students should limit the length of their presentations to thirty to sixty seconds to make sure that the presentations are to the point and do not include added distractions.

2. Students should locate the recording feature in the interactive whiteboard software.

3. When the groups are ready to present their presentations, have them press the Record button.

4. When a group has completed a short presentation, have the group click on the Record button again; as a result of that, the software automatically creates a video. Have each group complete this step.

5. Students should then upload their videos to Google Drive to share them.

Connections

You can apply this lesson to different content areas in the following suggested ways.

- **English language arts:** Students can create an instructional video about the parts of speech.

- **Mathematics:** Students can explain their thought process to a partner by creating an instructional video.

TEACHING TIPS

- For tips on creating videos, refer to chapter 1 (page 13).

- Students can practice their narration with a peer prior to recording.

- Students should rewatch their own videos to check for clarity.

- Creating instructional videos is a great way for English learners to practice fluency.

TECH TIPS

- In loud classroom environments, consider using headphones with a microphone or a standalone microphone while recording student narration.

- Model this recording process to the class first. Teachers will be able to show the students how the tools work, and students will see the bigger picture of the purpose of the lesson.

- **Science:** Students can record themselves drawing a model that shows the movement of a molecule through the water cycle.

Wow: Assisting Others' Learning With Instructional Videos

Learning goal:
I can create and share an instructional video or screencast to teach others.

This lesson goes beyond creating a video that simply explains student learning, as students now focus on how to create a step-by-step instructional guide for another learner to use. Students will need to think outside the box to bring in examples and descriptions that explain how and why each step occurs in the process. Students develop skills through this lesson that help them become critical thinkers and problem solvers who can successfully communicate their thought process with peers and the global community.

Process: Creating a Video Slideshow

Students work in groups to create a step-by-step instructional video. Instructional videos can be in different forms of media: a presentation such as a slideshow, a movie, or even a *screencast*.

A screencast is a recording of a device's screen with voice added to explain a concept. For example, students can create a video explaining how to properly put away computers at the end of class. Students can use many different types of technologies to create screencasts, and chapter 1 (page 33) includes more information on screencasting. In this lesson, students will make a video slideshow. To complete the following seven lesson steps, we recommend you use Animoto (https://animoto.com). If you prefer, you can adapt this process for use with a variety of other options. Other options include but are not limited to Adobe Spark (https://spark .adobe.com) and Slidely (https://slide.ly).

1. Create an Animoto education account at https:// animoto.com/education/classroom for your students.

2. Students will decide which classroom procedure they would like to make a video slideshow about and brainstorm the steps required in this procedure.

3. Have students log in to the provided Animoto account.

4. Tell students to choose a theme and music and then insert text and pictures based on project requirements.

5. Students record their voice as they talk through the steps of the concept. They should clearly state the objective of the video in the introduction. Limit instructional videos to thirty seconds to one minute in length.

6. Have students rewatch their videos to make sure they state their objective clearly and explain each step correctly.

7. Students should publish their project and submit its URL to the class LMS. You can publish these videos on the school or classroom website for the students' classmates to use when they need reminders of classroom procedures and tasks.

Connections

You can apply this lesson to different content areas in the following suggested ways.

- **English language arts:** Students can create instructional videos about writing a three-paragraph essay and then share their videos with students in the grade below them. This will help build on the writing process for each grade.

- **Social science:** After students create their instructional videos, have them share their work with another class in the district. Students can create the instructional videos about something that pertains to the standards in their grade level. For example, in grades 3–5, students can create instructional videos about explorers' travels to the New World.

- **Science:** Students can create videos to clarify the proper use of tools in an investigation. You can publish these videos for their classmates to use, or you can show them before the beginning of a lab.

- **Music:** Have students create instructional videos about how to play an instrument and share the videos with other classes in the building.

TEACHING TIPS

▸ Students should plan out their presentation before using the technology. Students can write a script before they use the technology.

▸ Practicing with a peer before recording helps students create a clear message.

TECH TIPS

▸ Refer to chapter 1 (page 33) for information about video and screencast creation.

▸ Many video slideshow creation websites, such as Animoto, allow you to insert your own videos to create a completed project. Consider using the built-in camera that comes with your device to record these videos.

Connecting With a Variety of Audiences

Not only is being a creative communicator and global collaborator part of ISTE's (2016) student standards, but connecting with a variety of audiences teaches students 21st century skills and gives them a larger purpose for their hard work. This section will lead you through a series of lessons where students first connect with classmates, then with peers, and eventually, in the wow level, with a global audience. Giving students the opportunity to connect with people outside of their school allows them to see how their learning can have a large impact on others.

Novice: Connecting With Classmates

Providing students with the opportunity to share a visual and description of a topic with their peers is the purpose of this lesson. Students can connect with classmates digitally using a variety of formats, including shared files on Google Drive, and on class forums and virtual spaces such as Padlet. Students will also share their instructional video from the previous lessons through the classroom LMS. Students can use the content skills learned to deepen and expand their interest in and understanding of the topic.

Process: Communicating With Classmates Using a Shared Document

To complete the following four lesson steps, we recommend you use Google Docs (https://docs.google.com), the word processing app in Google Drive. If you prefer, you can adapt this process for use with a variety of other options. There are a variety of other tools that allow for online collaboration within Google, such as Google Slides (www.google.com/slides/about), Google Sheets (www.google.com/intl/en_us/sheets/about), and Google Sites (https://sites.google.com). Outside of Google, students and teachers may want to collaborate using Padlet (https://padlet.com), an app and website that allows anyone with the link to post text and pictures to a shared online board.

Learning goal:
I can connect with my classroom peers online.

1. Have one student open up his or her Google Drive and click on New > Google Docs. This opens up a new document.

2. Have the student create a title for the document and then click on the Share button. The student should select Anyone With the Link Can Edit.

3. The student should then share the link to the document on the discussion board in the class LMS so the rest of the class can access it.

4. On this shared document, have students collaborate with one another on projects and assignments in real time. For example, they can capture questions and discussions throughout a unit by recording their ideas in one Google Doc. Then all students can use this document to review for a summative assessment.

Connections

You can apply this lesson to different content areas in the following suggested ways.

- **English language arts:** Students can start by picking a book that they would like to recommend to their class. Next, they write a few sentences about why other students in their class should read this book. Students take a *book shelfie*—a picture of them holding the book. Encourage them to creatively take it. Students then post the picture along with their recommendation to the class Padlet (https://padlet.com). Students can then view the Padlet whenever they want to read a book a classmate recommends.

- **Mathematics:** Students can work together on analyzing data in a shared Google Sheet. Students can import data and create graphs together online. Different roles can be assigned to different students. For example, students might have different data that they have to collect, but use everyone's data in a final comparison graph. By keeping all of the data together on one Google Sheet, all students will have access to edit and manipulate as needed.

- **Social science:** Students can work in groups to collaborate online in a shared Google Slide to create presentations to summarize the key details in a social science unit. As an extension, other students in the class can use these videos to prepare for a summative assessment.

- **Science:** Have students discuss an essential scientific question or scientific principle by collaborating on a shared Padlet.

Operational: Connecting With Peers

This lesson focuses on providing students with an opportunity to write to a broader audience beyond the walls of the classroom. Students explain their understanding as well as challenge others to learn and think deeply. The skills learned from this lesson provide students with an opportunity to share their learning to positively impact the learning of peers throughout their school.

Process: Using Presentation Software to Communicate

To complete the following three lesson steps, we recommend you use Google Slides (www.google.com/slides/about), the presentation app within Google Drive. If you prefer, you can adapt this process for use with a variety of other options. There are many other options within Google that allow peers to communicate online. Options include but are not limited to Google Sheets (www.google.com/intl/en_us/sheets/about), Google Docs (https://docs.google.com), and Google Sites (https://sites.google.com). Outside of Google, some online collaboration tools include Padlet (https://padlet.com) and Stormboard (https://stormboard.com). These sites allow students to post a small amount of text or pictures whereas Google applications allow for more in-depth learning.

1. Create a new presentation in Google Slides, and click on the Share button at the top of the presentation. The whole class works on the same presentation, so share the document by selecting Anyone With the Link Can Edit. Share this link on the announcements or discussion section of the class LMS.

Learning goal:
I can connect with students in other classrooms online.

2. In this shared presentation, students can collaborate with one another in real time. Have students pick the slides that they will work on and identify them with their names. Each student will work on one slide. Students will claim a slide as their responsibility in the project by adding to the slide they choose a text box with their name on it. This allows students to work as productively as possible and not erase another student's work. Students should then complete their slide with the necessary information. Once they feel that their slide is finished, they will have the ability to give feedback to their peers' slides.

3. The Comments feature embedded within Google Slides allows students to comment on another person's work and ask for clarification or suggest ideas.

Connections

You can apply this lesson to different content areas in the following suggested ways.

- **English language arts:** A teacher can create a Google Slide with a different character on each slide from a read-aloud story. The teacher can share the Google Slide with the class or school, and students can type a character trait on the slides. As the slides get populated with ideas, students learn from each other and develop a stronger understanding of the characters.

- **Social science:** When students study geography and culture, have them use shared slides like Google Slides as a collaborative tool to connect with another classroom to learn about different places in the world. A teacher can create a Google Slide with a question on each slide about the geography or culture in the location of the classroom they are connecting with. Students will work on the slides to answer the questions and add pictures to help share about where they live. Pose questions via the shared Google Slides such as: How does geography affect human life where you live? What do you do outside

TEACHING TIPS

▸ Consider making an example slide at the beginning of the shared presentation that the class will be collaborating on. Students can then use your slide as a model when making their own, so that all information is accounted for.

▸ Google Slides is a fantastic tool for collaborating on a presentation. However, if you want your class to collaborate online with peers for brainstorming purposes, consider using Padlet or Stormboard, which limit the text that students can write.

in the winter where you live? What is the highest point where you live? and How much rain falls where you live?

- **Science:** You, as the teacher, can connect with another classroom so the two classrooms can collaborate on a shared Google Slides presentation on a specific topic, such as different weather and climates found throughout the world. When the two classes complete the presentation, they can present it to a third classroom.

- **English learners:** Have students collaborate on shared Google Slides. The teacher can create the slides with different vocabulary words. Students then are assigned a slide and edit the slide to include a picture of the word and the translation of the word. When the presentation is finished, each student will have access to an online set of flashcards.

Wow: Connecting With a Global Audience

Learning goal:
I can connect with a global audience through social media.

This lesson focuses on sharing student learning beyond the walls of a school building. Sharing student work on a social media site and inviting input from the larger community provide students with a firsthand opportunity to see how their learning impacts others. It is important for students to understand the power of social media and how to use it in a positive way. While there are age restrictions on social media sites, the authors have found other ways in this lesson that allow students to access the power of social media without breaking any age-restriction standards. Students can apply the skills learned during this closely guided lesson on the many social media sites that they have and will have available for consumer use.

Process: Sharing Student Work on Social Media

Twitter (https://twitter.com) is a popular social media site for communicating through text and multimedia. This great tool allows educators and students alike to connect globally. Because of Twitter's minimum-age requirement of thirteen years old, we encourage the use of a teacher or classroom account so students under the age of thirteen can still reap the benefits of the global Twitter community. If you set up a teacher or classroom account, students can send you what they would like to post and then sign the approved post with their initials. Be sure to check with your administrator before posting student work online to see if they would like you to send out a separate permission form for parents to sign. To complete the following three lesson steps, we recommend you use Twitter (https://twitter.com). If you prefer, you can adapt this process for use with a variety of other options. Other options for how your students communicate their posts to you (in addition to the Google Doc option referenced in this lesson), include creating a Google Form for students to submit their posts, using pencil and paper, or even submitting through a discussion post on your LMS platform. There are also a variety of social media outlets that you can create classroom accounts on besides Twitter. Choose a social media account that best suits your classroom and community needs, whether that be Twitter, Facebook, Instagram, Snapchat, and so on.

1. Open Google Docs (https://docs.google.com), and demonstrate to students the word count feature in the Tools menu. This is a great tool for students to know about because all tweets must have 140 characters or fewer. It is important to have the students start in Google Docs instead of Twitter itself, in order to abide by the age restrictions within Twitter.

2. Students can then post their tweets in Google Docs and sign with their initials. The teacher can then review the tweets and post them to the classroom Twitter account. The classroom account will then show all of the students' writing and thoughts without having them actually access Twitter itself.

3. As a class, the teacher can then view a posted tweet on the smart board or other projector and watch the tweet activity. Click on the tweet that the teacher posted in the classroom account to open it and see the number of impressions and the number of total engagements made with the tweet. This is a built-in Twitter feature that shows how many people have seen the tweet (impressions), and the total

TEACHING TIPS

▸ Students should have voice and choice when selecting the appropriate technology tool for the task.

▸ You can create a Google Form that limits the number of characters it allows in order to mirror the character limit on Twitter. You can then copy and paste tweet submissions into a post on the class Twitter account. This is slightly different than a Google Doc because it allows students to just submit one "tweet" or response on the form at a time. This process mirrors the actual process in Twitter more accurately.

▸ Teach students about how hashtags allow posts to reach a broader audience. See page 12 in the introduction for a discussion of hashtags.

engagements refers to how many people engaged with the post (for example, liked the post, shared the post, or commented on the post). These analytics have power in teaching students the extent of the global community.

Connections

You can apply this lesson to different content areas in the following suggested ways.

- **English language arts:** Students can create a Prezi (https://prezi.com) about the story elements of a book they have read and publish it to the Prezi online community. Students can then interact with the global community through views and comments.

- **Mathematics:** Students can post a mathematics question on Twitter through a teacher-created account and analyze the answers collected.

- **Social science:** A class can create a survey about its community and post the survey to the school website to collect data from community members.

- **Art:** Students can take pictures of their artwork and post them to the school website to reach a global audience.

Collaborating and Giving Feedback

Collaboration goes beyond just sharing a product with someone. Collaboration is the act of working together to create a product that improves with the interaction between two or more people. In this section, the authors note the power of giving and utilizing feedback and how to incorporate this into your classroom. The lessons work through a series of giving and receiving feedback, from starting just within your classroom to collaborating and giving and receiving feedback on a global scale. Students will begin to explore the strength in numbers and the knowledge of experts, broaden their perspectives, and work effectively in teams in the online community.

TECH TIPS

- Decide on your class's objective or goal when choosing another classroom to collaborate with, considering age, location, and time zone.

- Discuss with students the importance of online safety. Many online discussion forums are public, and students should take precautions with what they share with another class.

- Model how to appropriately interact online, using appropriate language and grammar.

- Consider connecting with another school in your district to practice collaborating beyond the walls of the classroom before you bring in an outside expert.

- English learners can type a paper in Google Docs and use the translate feature to change the language to share the paper with a parent who does not speak English. While this tool sometimes produces inaccurate, even comical, translations, it is improving each day. Even if the translation isn't perfect, it might help some parents understand what is happening in the classroom.

Novice: Giving and Receiving Feedback

In this lesson, students have an opportunity to work on an online document that allows the teacher to view their work and give immediate feedback. The purpose of this lesson is to give students a safe environment in which to learn online and learn from the feedback that they receive.

Process: Interacting on a Video Site

To complete the following five lesson steps, we recommend you use PlayPosit (www.playposit.com), a free interactive website that allows teachers to post instructional videos while embedding questions throughout to receive feedback and give immediate feedback to their students. If you prefer, you can adapt this process for use with a variety of other options. Options include but are not limited to Classkick (www.class kick.com) and Formative (https://goformative.com).

1. Create a free account on the PlayPosit website, and then create a roster of the students in the class.

2. Create an instructional video and upload it to the website, or locate an existing instructional video. PlayPosit allows teachers to choose if they would like to create their own videos or use a premade instructional video from their website. PlayPosit offers more than four hundred thousand instructional interactive videos ready for all teachers to access. In PlayPosit, the teacher should click the Design Video Bulb button in the middle of the screen. From there, the teacher can choose one of Playposit's premade videos by clicking Browse Premade. To upload a video he or she created, the teacher simply copies the URL link from the video into the Video URL field under the heading that says "Know which video to use?" and then clicks Continue. The video will then upload automatically into PlayPosit's interactive program.

3. After uploading the video, the teacher can add questions throughout the video that will pop up as the students watch. At any point in the video, the teacher can click pause and then click the Add Question button. This will add the question at

Learning goal:
I can collaborate with my teacher and use feedback.

TEACHING TIPS

▸ Model this process of receiving feedback on PlayPosit and using it to change your method of thinking on the board as a whole-group minilesson prior to having students do this individually. By modeling the process, students will understand the importance of utilizing the feedback to change their thinking.

▸ Clearly state the academic objective or goal of online work before focusing on the technology.

▸ Guide students on how you want them to provide feedback. For example, tell them if they should give constructive criticism, just answer questions, or give compliments.

▸ Discuss learning norms with students and how they can differ by location and classroom.

▸ Discuss with students that an author will not find all feedback useful.

TECH TIPS

▶ Prior to using PlayPosit or any similar program in the classroom, make sure to test your videos and questions on the device that students will be using. For example, if you create your video on a laptop but your students will be viewing and interacting on a tablet, make sure that the program runs smoothly on the student device.

▶ Consider exploring the advanced features of PlayPosit or similar programs if you feel comfortable. Some of these programs offer valuable data analysis tools.

exactly that point in the video, so as students are watching the instructional video, it pauses and asks these questions throughout. You have the option to add multiple-choice, free-response, or reflective-pause questions. If you choose to upgrade to the premium version, PlayPosit has additional options for question types.

4. Once you have completed all questions, click on Finish, and then the site provides a link you can use to share the video with students on the class LMS.

5. Place students into small groups to watch and answer the questions embedded in the video. As the students watch the videos and complete the questions embedded throughout, the teacher will be able to see their answers. The students will get automatic feedback to their answers from PlayPosit as well and can adjust their processes based on the feedback they receive. For example, if students answer a question wrong, PlayPosit will provide an example or additional video and ask another similar question before the students can move on.

Connections

You can apply this lesson to different content areas in the following suggested ways.

- **English language arts:** The teacher will upload a graphic organizer on story elements into Classkick. Students will complete the graphic organizer online. The teacher can provide immediate feedback to the students through Classkick, allowing them to correct any errors and have a better understanding of the story elements.

- **Mathematics:** The teacher can upload an instructional video on how to multiply fractions on PlayPosit. Students will answer questions embedded throughout the video. Students will receive feedback on their answers in order to best understand the new content and process immediately.

- **Science:** The teacher will upload an instructional video on the scientific method into PlayPosit.

Students will watch the video and answer questions that are embedded throughout the video. Students will receive immediate feedback on their answers through PlayPosit.

Operational: Collaborating With Peers

In this lesson, students will collaborate with peers in their classroom through a discussion board. It is important to teach students how to share their work with others in an online community but also how to give and receive feedback as well. By having the teacher create a safe place for students to share their work and interact with others, the teacher is beginning to meet ISTE standard 2b, which states, "Students engage in positive, safe, legal and ethical behavior when using technology, including social interactions online or when using networked devices" (ISTE, 2016).

Process: Creating Digital Portfolios

To complete the following four lesson steps, we recommend you use Seesaw (http://web.seesaw.me), a student-directed digital portfolio website and app that has free and premium features. Seesaw has many different features that allow students to have individual work portfolios, but this lesson will only focus on the class discussion wall feature. This feature allows students to share their work online in a safe environment. Only other students from the class will be able to view it. The class discussion wall also provides a safe place for students to comment on each other's work and start to learn the process of giving feedback as well as receiving feedback. Other aspects in Seesaw provide a great way to showcase student work with families and the global community. If you prefer, you can adapt this process for use with a variety of other options. Options for tools that allow students to post their work and give and receive feedback include but are not limited to Google Slides (www.google.com/slides/about), Google Docs (http://docs.google.com), and Schoology (www.schoology.com) or other LMS platforms.

1. Teachers create a free Seesaw account at https://web.seesaw.me, or log in through their Google accounts. When the teacher creates a new account, a short tutorial will pop up. Proceed through the tutorial,

Learning goal:
I can collaborate with students in my classroom and use feedback.

and then a "Create your class" screen will pop up. The teacher then names the class and clicks the grade level. This will generate a QR code that students will use to log in. Then, he or she will click the green check mark in the upper right-hand corner and will then be prompted to enter in all of the students' names in the class and click the green check mark when finished.

2. Students will then use the QR code provided to log in to Seesaw. Students will scan the QR code with any device that they are using in the class.

3. Once logged in, students can post photos, videos, or drawings to the class discussion wall. Students can share their writing through one of these features by using the option to add a note beneath the item, writing a description of the item or the process of completing the task depicted in an image or video. Make sure students get teacher approval for any items that they add to the class wall.

4. Students should like and comment on each other's work and provide feedback.

Connections

You can apply this lesson to different content areas in the following suggested ways.

- **English language arts:** Students can work together to share their opinions on a topic. They write opinion pieces in Seesaw and receive feedback from their peers and teacher.

- **Mathematics:** The teacher poses a multiplication problem on the board and has students solve the problem in any way that they can. Students post their strategies and solutions on the class discussion board in Seesaw. Other students comment and provide feedback on their work.

- **Social science:** Students can complete a project on their community and ask for feedback from their peers on what areas they suggest to explore further.

- **Science:** The teacher asks students to create a hypothesis on the experiment they are about to perform and has students post the hypothesis on the discussion board in Seesaw. Students comment and give feedback to each other on their posts.

- **Art:** Students can create a slide show presentation of artwork in Google Slides, and during the presentation, other students can use the Comments feature to post questions about perspective, point of view, mood, and so on.

Wow: Collaborating Globally

This lesson provides students with an opportunity to use a global audience to obtain feedback about a specific topic. The purpose of this lesson is to have a discussion with a broader audience to collect a variety of viewpoints on the topic. Communication and collaboration skills learned during this activity will provide students with the confidence and ability to feel comfortable to look beyond books and websites for information and to bring in real-world stories they gain from global interactions to strengthen the authenticity of their projects.

Process: Connecting to a Global Audience Through a Blog

To complete the following two lesson steps, we recommend you use Blogger (www.blogger.com), Google's free blogging platform. Blogger is easy to use and packed with features, including the ability to leave comments for a blog's author. If you prefer, you can adapt this process for use with a variety of other options. Other options for websites that students can use to blog include but are not limited to Kidblog (https://kidblog.org/home) and WordPress (https://wordpress.com).

1. The teacher or the students can post student work on a classroom blog using Blogger. If the teacher wants the class blog to reach a broader audience, he or she can then post a link to the classroom blog on any social media outlet.

2. Students receive feedback from this global audience through the blog's commenting feature and use that feedback to enhance their future work.

Learning goal:
I can collaborate with a global audience and use feedback.

TEACHING TIPS

▸ Have students practice giving and receiving feedback with each other on the blog prior to sending the blog out to a more global community. This allows students to better understand how to utilize their feedback to make the biggest impact on their work.

▸ Consider sending the blog to another classroom in a different school, state, or country. Students will love connecting with others, and by communicating back and forth, they will learn so much from each other.

Connections

You can apply this lesson to different content areas in the following suggested ways.

- **English language arts:** Students can create pieces of writing that they share on a classroom blog. Using this blog, students receive feedback from a global audience.

- **Mathematics:** Students can solve a word problem and create a video of their work. They post their video on a classroom blog and receive feedback from their classmates.

- **Social science:** Students can complete a project about a region of the United States and ask for feedback from people who live in that area via a post on the classroom blog.

- **Science:** Students can complete projects on weather and biomes. They share their work on Blogger or a similar classroom blog, asking their audience members what types of weather they experience.

- **Art:** Students can discuss certain elements of a famous art piece on a classroom blog. Students can provide feedback to each other on their posts about the elements of the art piece they noticed.

Conclusion

We authors are all Twitter users who feel very comfortable connecting beyond the classroom walls because we know it works with our students. When a tweet comes back from across the globe, students feel empowered because they see their work really has importance. We love to watch our students study the analytics or data behind their tweets. When students run into school on Monday morning asking how many retweets their post got, you know you have engaged them. Teachers do not always think about engaging students with an authentic audience beyond the walls of the classroom when they plan lessons, but these types of activities are important. Such practices represent our students' future, and our job as educators is to get them ready for the world outside of school. We will watch our #NOWClassrooms hashtag to see what your students create, how they collaborate, and how you communicate their learning online.

DISCUSSION QUESTIONS

Consider the following questions for personal reflection or in collaborative work with colleagues.

▸ What purpose does having students create instructional videos serve?

▸ How would you describe *flipped learning* to someone who has never heard that term?

▸ What is one video tool you would like to explore in more depth, and why?

▸ Why is connecting beyond the walls of the classroom important?

▸ Why do teachers need to provide feedback to students, and what is an effective way to communicate this feedback with all students?

▸ Why do students need to provide feedback to each other, and how do you plan on teaching this?

▸ What is one example of a lesson in this chapter you could expand to connect with a broader audience?

▸ Which online collaborative platform in this chapter do you feel will work best with your students, and why?

▸ What is one technology tool from this chapter you will share with your colleagues?

▸ What lesson in this chapter do you find the most interesting, and why do you feel that way?

Conducting Research and Curating Information

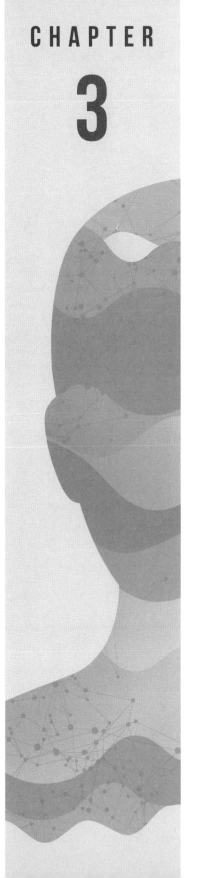

The 21st century classroom already comes equipped with students who know how to quickly look up answers on any technology device. Looking up a single answer no longer poses as much of a challenge to students as it did in the early 2000s. However, students need to learn how to do research at a level beyond finding basic facts to become college and career ready. According to Nell K. Duke (2016), "Studies suggest that many U.S. students are too trusting of information found on the internet and rarely evaluate the credibility of a website's information." Modeling, discussion, and demonstration all play key parts in helping students learn how to identify and use legitimate information found on websites. By teaching research skills specifically through modeling, discussion, and demonstration, students will soon become masters in independently conducting research.

In this chapter, we have developed a series of lessons to guide the third- through fifth-grade teacher through lessons that prepare students to identify and use quality online sources. By working through these lessons, students will fulfill ISTE (2016) knowledge constructor standards for which students

> plan and employ effective research strategies to locate information and other resources for their intellectual or creative

pursuits . . . evaluate the accuracy, perspective, credibility and relevance of information, media, data, or other resources . . . [and] curate information from digital resources using a variety of tools and methods to create collections of artifacts that demonstrate meaningful connections or conclusions. (ISTE, 2016)

Cathy Knutson (2014) powerfully states, "Informal research, with children seeking to answer their own questions, is engaging, motivating and empowering." We encourage sharing of documents and projects both within and outside of school to further motivate and excite students about the quality of the final product. The lessons we offer will support teachers as they help students learn critical information-literacy skills and understand how asking the right question will help them determine the validity of the content they find on websites. They cover the tasks of gathering information and evaluating information. Students will learn how to locate information using age-appropriate search engines in order to participate in shared research with guidance. For information about the tools we mention in these lessons, and for clarity on technology terms you may encounter in this chapter, see the appendix on page 133. Visit **go.SolutionTree.com/technology** to download a free reproducible version of this appendix and to access live links to the tools mentioned in this book.

Gathering Information

In this section of the book, lessons help students begin to unlock the power of research and all of the information that can be found on the Internet. However, it is important that students learn how to conduct research online both appropriately and efficiently. These lessons guide teachers and students through a series of ideas for teaching students how to gather information from the web, starting with providing students with a list of sources, to gathering information from a familiar website, to finally gathering information from a search engine. The goal of these lessons is to make all students independent researchers.

Novice: Gathering Information From a List of Sources

This lesson focuses on gathering information online from a teacher-generated list of sources. The purpose of this lesson is to introduce online research to students through safe and valid web sources so they develop critical information-literacy skills needed in grades 3–5 and in the future. Students will begin to recognize similarities among safe and valid web sources with the intent to eventually build up their knowledge to do research on their own through a search engine.

Process: Synthesizing Research in an Interactive Map

To complete the following six lesson steps, we recommend you use Google My Maps (www.google.com/maps/d). Google My Maps allows users to create their own maps and insert place markers with additional data about the locations. In this lesson, students will gather information about specific locations using a list of websites the teacher provides. The students will then take their research one step further by culminating the research in a map they create. If you prefer, you can adapt this process for use with a variety of other options, such as Padlet or Thinglink, using an image of a map as the background. This lesson works best if the teacher ties a learning objective to a geographical area, for example, the location of an event in history or the various locations included in a book.

1. Before the lesson, prepare a graphic organizer for students to record what they learn as they conduct research. This graphic organizer can be designed in any way that best fits both your students' needs and your learning objective. For example, if studying the Revolutionary War, students can list five significant locations related to the war and record facts about these locations.

2. Teachers should research websites that are age appropriate, accurate, and reliable that tie in with the learning objective. They should create a list of these websites and post them to the class LMS.

3. Have students open the class LMS and navigate to the websites you have listed to find the information about their topic. Students should

Learning goal:
I can use appropriate sources from a teacher-generated list.

TEACHING TIPS

▶ Set a specific content objective for students' information gathering, keeping in mind why students use the websites and what the goal of the research is.

▶ Consider using a fill-in-the-blank-type template for beginning research. For example, instead of just a blank table, consider scaffolding students' research by asking them to find the answers to specific questions.

navigate to multiple sources listed to complete their graphic organizers.

4. Once the graphic organizer is completed, have students go to the website Google My Maps and click on Create a New Map. Then have them click on the Add Marker icon and place markers on a map that identify the geographical areas they have researched.

5. Students can add information and photos from their research to their markers to share what they have learned about the given topic.

6. When finished, students can share the link to their map with you through the discussion or announcement section of the class LMS.

Connections

You can apply this lesson to different content areas in the following suggested ways.

- **English language arts:** Students will research a historical event that took place in the novel they have read. The teacher will give them a list of websites to use for the research and a graphic organizer to fill out.

- **Science, technology, engineering, and mathematics (STEM):** Students can research different aspects of bridge design using two or three age-appropriate websites you provide, recording the different aspects in a graphic organizer. Provide students with a photo of a bridge, and have students highlight and annotate the different aspects of the bridge that they learned about in their research.

- **Social science:** Students can research a historical event and use multiple links the teacher provides to explain what events in history led up to this event. For example, what events in history happened that led to Martin Luther King Jr.'s "I Have a Dream" speech.

- **Science:** Students can fill out a graphic organizer with their research about an inventor and his or her invention from a list of sources you provide.

Operational: Gathering Information Through a Familiar Website

The goal of this lesson is to further students' research skills through focused Internet research. This lesson allows students to practice gathering information online without having to find their own safe and valid websites. These research skills are critical to all learners. Great free sites for students to use (though some have paid features) include:

- TweenTribune (www.tweentribune.com)

- Newsela (https://newsela.com)

- YouTube (www.youtube.com)

- KidzSearch (www.kidzsearch.com)

- KidRex (www.kidrex.org)

- BrainPOP (www.brainpop.com)

- Online encyclopedias, such as Encyclopaedia Britannica (www.britannica.com), Academic Kids (http://academickids.com), myON (www.myon .com), and many others

Process: Compiling Research Sources in Symbaloo

To complete the following six lesson steps, we recommend you use Symbaloo (www.symbaloo.com), a visually appealing social bookmarking website. Create a class page on Symbaloo to organize all the research tools students need to access. If you prefer, you can adapt this process for use with a variety of other options. Other options available for students to access information from include but are not limited to BrainPOP (www.brainpop.com) and myON (www.myon.com).

1. Assign a topic, such as animal life cycles, for students to research.

2. Navigate to the Symbaloo site to set up an account.

3. Click on the + tab. Then, under Add an Empty Webmix, type a name for the Symbaloo and click Add. Add research sites to create a visual compilation (webmix) of websites. By giving students access to the Symbaloo, you will give them access to all the websites that you add into the webmix.

Learning goal:
I can use a familiar website to research a topic.

TEACHING TIPS

▸ You can provide different types of graphic organizers based on student need. If a student needs more scaffolding, consider using a graphic organizer that asks specific questions. If a student needs less scaffolding, consider using a graphic organizer with more open-ended questions.

▸ Allow students to pick their favorite website from a list of choices on Symbaloo to complete their project. Remember student voice and choice are important during the information-collecting process and in how they present their final project.

4. Click on an empty tile to add a website that students can use for their research. Add the URL, name the tile, pick a color for the tile, and then click on Save.

5. Continue to add websites as you determine they are appropriate for research.

6. Post the Symbaloo on the class LMS for students to access at any time. Students will then navigate between the different websites posted on the Symbaloo to complete their research. Students can record their research in a notebook or on a graphic organizer you provide.

Connections

You can apply this lesson to different content areas in the following suggested ways.

- **English language arts:** Have students brainstorm ideas that interest them. Each student picks a topic to research and writes an argumentative essay either for or against the topic.

- **Mathematics:** Using a familiar website, such as Khan Academy (www.khanacademy.org), have students research different strategies for solving a multiplication problem. Have them record the different strategies they find in a graphic organizer.

- **Social science:** Given a historical event, students can conduct online research to create a multimedia presentation, sharing the event from the perspective of a person who participated in the event.

- **Science:** Students can research and investigate a solution to a problem (such as preventing the impact of severe weather, converting energy, or protecting Earth's resources) from a teacher-provided list of websites.

- **Music:** Have students research musicians from a historical era.

Wow: Gathering Information Through a Search Engine

This lesson focuses on students gathering information through an age-appropriate search engine. The purpose of this lesson is for students to learn how to find safe and reliable websites on their own and use these websites to answer questions and become critical problem solvers. Students must know how to do research on their own and identify what sources will provide them with accurate and reliable information.

Process: Conducting a Voice and Choice Research Project

To complete the following four lesson steps, we recommend you use KidRex (www.kidrex.org), a safe search engine for students. If you prefer, you can adapt this process for use with a variety of other options. Some other options include but are not limited to Safe Search Kids (www.safesearchkids .com) and KidzSearch (www.kidzsearch.com).

1. As a whole class, brainstorm a list of problems that exist in your community (such as recyclable objects being thrown out, high stress levels due to testing, and so on). From generated ideas, students pick a topic they feel passionate about. The students will research how they can help solve this problem in the community.

2. The teacher creates a graphic organizer that students will fill out with their research. The graphic organizer should be a general guide since each group of students will be researching a different problem. For example, the graphic organizer can ask the students what problem they are researching, statistics about the problem, solutions that the community has already tried or are in place now, solutions that are working in different communities, and what they are going to implement to help the problem in their own community.

3. Students navigate to KidRex and begin to research their topic and complete their graphic organizer.

4. Have students create a final project to present to the community to help solve the problem they are

Learning goal:

I can use an age-appropriate search engine to locate resources.

TEACHING TIPS

▸ You may want to complete this entire project on your own prior to starting the lesson with your students. This way, you can show them what each step looks like as you go. It will also provide clarity on what kind of information students will need to be looking for while researching.

▸ Have the students check in with you after they choose their problem to research. Make sure that the problems are something that an in-depth Internet search can provide some solutions to.

researching. Students should give examples from their research about why this is a problem and why they think their solution will work.

Connections

You can apply this lesson to different content areas in the following suggested ways.

- **English language arts:** Students can design a question about an event in a biography they read and then research the question's topic using age-appropriate search engines.

- **STEM:** Students can research design components related to their topic of study. Example topics include solutions for the impact of weather-related hazards; energy conversion to protect Earth's resources; and more effective sporting protection, equipment, and tools. Based on their research, students design a prototype to address the issue they research, test it, and then redesign it and start the process again on another topic.

- **Social science:** Students can take a historical topic and research its impact or how it has been impacted throughout time. Example topics include how primitive tools differ from modern tools, how clothing has changed during different historical periods, and how Native Americans have adapted and changed over time to survive.

- **Art:** Students can research how art has evolved over time and the part it has played in history.

Evaluating Information

ISTE (2016) student standard 3b states that students need to be able to "evaluate the accuracy, perspective, credibility and relevance of information, media, data or other resources." While the Internet provides a wealth of knowledge to all students, it is often filled with misinformation as well. It is an important skill for students to be able to identify a reliable source for information on the web. These lessons will guide students through recognizing aspects of a reliable source to identifying the purpose of a website, and eventually lead students to be able to independently find a reliable source on their own.

Novice: Identifying Aspects of a Reliable Source

The purpose of this lesson is for students to determine what makes a website reliable. Students start by evaluating a website that the teacher has already deemed reliable because it gives them a good base of knowledge to further their skill. Eventually, students can do research through a search engine and determine on their own the reliability of sources.

Process: Recognizing Fact and Opinion

To complete the following four lesson steps, we recommend you use TweenTribune (www.tweentribune.com), a current-events website for tweens that features articles organized by reading level. If you prefer, you can adapt this process for use with a variety of other options. Some options include but are not limited to Newsela (https://newsela.com) and Scholastic News (http://magazines.scholastic.com).

1. Have students navigate to TweenTribune and locate the article that they will be analyzing. Have students highlight facts and opinions in the article. Ask them to consider how the facts or opinions add to or take away from the reliability of the source.

2. Next, have students navigate to a website that contains age-appropriate content but is *not* a reliable source (for example, includes many opinions, bias, or discrimination). Have the students highlight the facts and opinions on this webpage.

3. Create a T-chart as a class to compare the article and website as you discuss information and categorize it as fact or opinion.

4. Use what you discussed with students about the TweenTribune article to help students identify facts and opinions when looking at an entire webpage.

Learning goal:
I can identify aspects of a reliable website that the teacher provides.

TEACHING TIPS

▸ Identify different websites for students to explore.

▸ Refer to the appendix (page 133) to locate age-appropriate search engines.

TECH TIPS

▸ If you have a projector, an iPad, or another device that has a split-screen capability, consider pulling up two websites at the same time and comparing and contrasting the information on each of the websites with students.

▸ If your students' devices do not allow them to highlight a webpage, consider downloading an application, such as LINER (http://getliner.com) that will allow them to do so.

Connections

You can apply this lesson to different content areas in the following suggested ways.

- **English language arts:** Compare and contrast two persuasive articles found on the Internet. Have students decide which article comes from a reliable source and which article does not. Use these articles and the reasoning behind the reliability to have students mirror the writing style when they write their own persuasive paragraphs.

- **Social science:** Review the Smithsonian websites *Smithsonian Magazine* (www.smithsonianmag.com) and Smithsonian Institution (www.si.edu), and the Library of Congress website (www.loc.gov), and have students look at the purposes of different web domains (such as *.edu*, *.com*, and *.gov*). Students should determine which would best serve the purpose of the research they do. Have students choose and scan articles from two different domains. The students should identify which article contains the needed information based on the facts or opinions stated in the articles and use the best article or articles for their research. Research can include but is not limited to American history, prehistoric climate change, and geography from space.

- **Science:** Use a .gov website and a .edu website based on space exploration (such as www.nasa.gov and http://space.edu), and have students determine which might act as a better resource for an assignment to gather information about the future of America's space program based on the quality of the facts presented on the site.

Operational: Determining the Purpose of a Website

Websites have many uses and purposes. For example, you can design a website to persuade, to sell something, to inform, or to provide images. The purpose of this lesson is for students to analyze a website and determine its purpose or use. This skill will help students further develop their skill

Learning goal:
I can evaluate a website to determine its use and purpose for research.

set for evaluating websites. If students can determine the purpose of a website, they get one step closer to determining the reliability of that source.

Process: Explaining Why a Website Is Research Worthy

To complete the following six lesson steps, we recommend you use KidzSearch (www.kidzsearch.com), an age-appropriate search engine students can use. If you prefer, you can adapt this process for use with a variety of other options. Other options include but are not limited to KidRex (www .kidrex.org) and Safe Search Kids (www.safesearchkids.com).

1. The teacher decides a topic that the class is going to research for the purpose of this lesson. For example, the teacher may have the class research climate change.

2. Have the students navigate to KidzSearch and type in the topic in the search box.

3. Make sure that students understand search results often start with advertisements, and point out what ads look like on various search engines. For example, where the advertisements appear on KidzSearch versus KidRex, and so on.

4. Have students pick a website from the search results and explain why they think they will find it useful for their research on a given topic.

5. Have students visit a different site from the search results to determine if it will help them in their research. If they do not find it useful for their purpose, they should check a different site in the search results until they find a site they can use.

6. Create a Google Slides presentation, and assign each student a slide on which to input the URLs for the websites he or she has chosen and explain why each website appropriately meets his or her research needs.

Connections

You can apply this lesson to different content areas in the following suggested ways.

- **English language arts:** Students can use a search engine to find websites that they can evaluate for information about a novel they study.

- **Social science:** Students can use a search engine to find websites that they can evaluate for information about historical events they study.

- **Science:** Students can use a search engine to find websites that they can evaluate for valid information about a science topic.

- **Music:** Students can compare and contrast information from various websites about famous composers they are doing research on.

Wow: Identifying a Reliable Source

During this lesson, students complete a research project without any assistance. By the end of this lesson, students will be able to identify a reputable and reliable online source independently. Students must gain the extremely important skill of identifying a reliable website. If students cannot do this, they could use invalid, biased, or incorrect information throughout their research. Students will use this skill throughout their school careers and beyond for all their future research needs.

Process: Creating Interactive Videos

To complete the following eight lesson steps, we recommend you use TouchCast (www.touchcast.com), a smart video production website and app for both Apple and Android devices that allows students to create and share interactive videos. TouchCast offers a free app for iPads and Android devices, and it also offers TouchCast for Education, which is a paid version with additional features. If you prefer, you can adapt this process for use with a variety of other options. Options for creating a video include but are not limited to iMovie (www.apple.com/imovie) and WeVideo (www.wevideo.com).

1. Choose a topic for students to research (for example, an event in history such as the Great Chicago Fire).

2. Students navigate to a kid-safe search engine such as KidRex and search the topic.

Learning goal:
I can identify a reputable, reliable source independently.

3. Students research information about the topic. However, throughout this process, students use skills from the previous lessons to determine if the websites are reliable. For example, a student needs to evaluate the website for facts or opinions, determine the purpose of the website, and so on.

4. Have students create a newscast or panel discussion to share the information they research.

5. Tell groups of students conducting research to share a Google Doc to organize their research and plan their final TouchCast presentation.

6. In TouchCast for Education, the teacher creates an account, and all the students are under the teacher.

7. Students open TouchCast and start to build the TouchCast story using the research they have collected. They can add text, video, and digital images all into one TouchCast presentation.

8. Students should share the final TouchCasts with the teacher through the classroom LMS.

Connections

You can apply this lesson to different content areas in the following suggested ways.

- **English language arts:** Students can research the setting of a book they read by finding websites using a search engine of their choice and then create a presentation. They evaluate the information they find to make sure their presentation is accurate and without bias.

- **Social science:** Students can research an event in history, comparing and contrasting different reliable sources' news accounts of it.

- **Science:** Students can research and validate information about renewable energy.

- **Physical education:** Students can conduct research about the various Olympic venues around the world and present reliable information using student voice and choice.

▸ Have students work with a partner to discuss the different websites that they found using the search engine.

▸ Provide students with age-appropriate, safe search engines to find the websites.

▸ Model effective searching using keywords.

⋯ DISCUSSION QUESTIONS

Consider the following questions for personal reflection or in collaborative work with colleagues.

▸ Why should you introduce online research to students by giving them a list of sources?

▸ How should you select research topics?

▸ Besides the step of collecting research, what else do you need to teach students in the process of identifying reliable resources?

▸ What is one example you can give of an age-appropriate search engine? Why should you use age-appropriate search engines with students?

▸ How can students identify a reliable website to collect research?

▸ Why should students compare and contrast information from various sources?

▸ What is bias, and how do you plan on teaching students about it?

▸ What is one research project you do that you would like to modify, and why?

▸ What importance do student voice and choice have in this chapter?

▸ What is one thing from this chapter you will share with colleagues?

Conclusion

This chapter addressed important basic research and evaluation skills students need to develop in the 21st century. Throughout the lessons in this chapter, students employed the four Cs of communication, collaboration, critical thinking, and creativity to learn these research skills and also present their research findings in creative, new ways. Every learner needs these essential information fluency skills. Although the Internet provides valuable knowledge to all users, it also has an abundance of unsubstantiated information or misinformation. It is important for students to be able to recognize the difference between reliable information and misinformation. Donald Leu, from the University of Connecticut, shows that many students that are considered native to the digital world have little critical evaluation skills of online material (Daily Mail Reporter, 2011). In Leu's research, many students believed his fake article about an endangered tree octopus as factual information (Daily Mail Reporter, 2011). This stresses the importance of teaching students academic research.

It is important for teachers to repeatedly model these skills. To be well-prepared digital citizens for the 21st century, students need to become evaluators of information, not just consumers of information, in all content areas.

Thinking Critically to Solve Problems

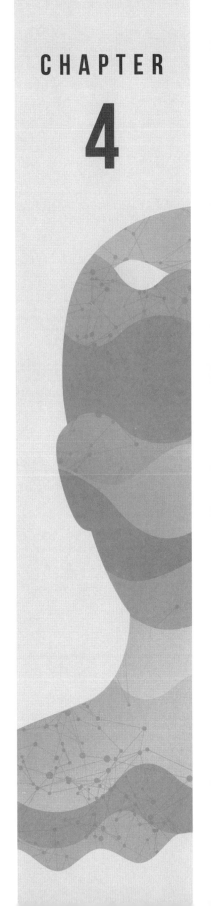

Students in the 21st century classroom need to become thinkers, dreamers, and problem solvers. It is vital to guide students through the process of effectively solving problems. Learning the difference between simply using a collaborative tool and actually collaborating with colleagues will create the problem solvers needed to move the world ahead in the 21st century and beyond. Preparing students to solve problems of the future that remain, as of yet, unknown to us involves creating a classroom in which students analyze data to plan and prepare, employing a variety of tools to demonstrate learning and understanding.

The lessons in this chapter equip students to create a plan to collect data. After that, students process the information in the data based on real-world needs. These lessons challenge students to think deeply and logically about the processes needed to solve many complex problems, tying in the four Cs of communication, collaboration, critical thinking, and creativity, which are all tied to the ISTE (2016) standards. Ultimately, teachers must help students understand that to solve a problem, they must collect and show data.

Joshua Block (2014) notes, "Learning that incorporates student choice provides a pathway for students to fully, genuinely invest themselves in quality work that matters. Participating in learning design allows students to make meaning of content on their own terms." ISTE (2016) standards encourage educators to provide students with lessons that incorporate innovative design and construct knowledge from the information that they gather. The lessons in this chapter provide these types of opportunities for student choice, asking students to show evidence of their learning by choosing a technology tool that effectively demonstrates their understanding of the various learning standards using innovative design programs. For information about the tools we mention in these lessons, and for clarity on technology terms you may encounter in this chapter, see the appendix on page 133. Visit **go.SolutionTree.com/technology** to download a free reproducible version of this appendix and to access live links to the tools mentioned in this book.

The first series of lessons in this chapter focuses on identifying and defining tasks for investigation. Teachers prompt students to select the best tool for each task and then explain why a tool is the best choice. The second series of lessons develops self-motivated learners as they begin to plan, design, and manage projects using online collaborative tools. Students use their voice and choice to find answers to real-world problems and then share the projects with an authentic audience to become global collaborators who can communicate with others in order to complete a task or solve a problem. This creates ownership of the projects and motivates students to follow through to completion. The final series of lessons focuses on finding data-driven solutions. These lessons guide students to develop their skills in data collection and analysis.

Evaluating and Choosing Digital Tools

Today's 21st century learners need to understand how to evaluate digital tools in order to pick the correct tool for the learning outcomes. As students grow as critical thinkers, they will begin to focus more on the content of projects rather than the tools to show their learning. The following lessons will help students learn to evaluate tools based on the properties the tools contain. They will also learn that it is important to reflect on what worked well when using a tool so that as they grow in experience, they will be more successful picking tools that will help them complete multiple tasks.

Novice: Selecting Digital Tools

In this lesson, students reflect on a teacher-directed lesson to identify the properties of digital tools that make them appropriate for a given task. The purpose of this lesson is to help students become proficient in their understanding of how to pick the proper digital tool for a task so that they can communicate their learning in a way that anyone who reviews their project can understand.

Process: Reflecting on the Appropriateness of Digital Tools

To complete the following four lesson steps, we recommend you use Formative (https://goformative.com), a free website for collecting data from students. Students can submit drawings, answer multiple-choice questions, or provide text as exit slips. If you prefer, you can adapt this process for use with a variety of other options. Options include but are not limited to the Question feature in Google Classroom (https://class room.google.com), a class discussion, and written reflections.

1. After finishing a project utilizing a specific digital tool, sign in to Formative with your Google account to post a question.

2. Click on New Assignment, and add a question as the title. Then, click Add a Question, and pick the appropriate type of question you'd like to ask the class about the effectiveness of the digital tool they used in the project.

3. Put in the question and the answer choice or choices, and then select the final answer if needed. Example questions include, Did you find this tool effective? Why did we pick this tool and not something else? What did you like about this tool? What would you change about this tool if you could change something? and What other uses do you think this tool has? This will enable students to reflect on the tools that they have used so that they can build a list of tools that will identify how

Learning goal:
I can explain why the selected digital tool is the most appropriate for the given task or problem.

TEACHING TIPS

▸ You can use a variety of formats for the reflection in this lesson. For example, you can use a class discussion, written documentation, or electronic responses. Please choose whatever format best suits your needs and your students' needs.

▸ To scaffold the assignment, you could give multiple questions to small groups and have students collaborate on an answer that they have come to a consensus on. Then they would share it with the class.

they have been effective or ineffective in the creative design process. This process will teach them what questions to ask themselves as they evaluate tools for future use.

4. Use the responses to guide a classroom discussion on the effectiveness of the digital tool that the class used to complete the project.

Connections

You can apply this lesson to different content areas in the following suggested ways. For the following lessons, work with students to determine what type of questions they think would be important to determine if a tool is right for a task. Students can then answer those questions to evaluate the lesson.

- **English language arts:** Students can create a presentation using Keynote for an informational writing unit and reflect on the pros and cons of using Keynote for their presentation.

- **Mathematics:** Students can use the camera app on the device they are using to create a video explanation of a mathematics problem. Then students reflect on the benefits of using the camera to record their explanations.

- **Social science:** Students can use TouchCast to create a multimedia presentation about a past president. Then students reflect on the positives and negatives of using TouchCast to demonstrate their knowledge.

- **Science:** Students can use Piktochart (https://piktochart.com) to create an infographic on the life cycle of an animal. Upon completion, students reflect on the usefulness of Piktochart for demonstrating their knowledge.

- **Art:** Students can use Twitter to reach out to artists to find out about specific types of art media. Afterward, students reflect on the usefulness of Twitter to reach out to these experts.

Operational: Defining the Properties of Digital Tools

Give students a list of options for project completion in this lesson. Students demonstrate their understanding of digital tools as they pick a tool and explain why they find it appropriate for the successful completion of their project. The purpose of having students understand their chosen tool is so they can become discerning about different tools and the purposes they serve. As students plan for existing projects, they become more proficient at independently picking the best technology tool for a task, given a limited number of choices.

Learning goal:

I can define why a digital tool selected from a list is the best option for a given task or problem.

Process: Determining the Best Tool for a Specific Purpose

To complete the following seven lesson steps, we recommend you use Dotstorming (https://dotstorming.com), a free app classrooms or groups of students can use to vote online, creating their own Dotstorming board. If you prefer, you can adapt this process for use with a variety of other options. Options include but are not limited to SurveyMonkey (www.surveymonkey.com), Plickers (https://plickers.com), Kahoot! (https://getkahoot.com), Quizizz (https://quizizz.com), or Google Forms (www.google.com/intl/en_us/forms/about).

1. Create a free account, and click on Add a Topic. The topic could read, "What digital tool do you think is best for making a presentation?"

2. Add answer options by clicking on Add an Idea. Answer options should be based on the items the class determined were important in the previous lesson. Answers could include: easy to use, saves automatically, has premade templates, is engaging and fun, has pictures in the program, or others.

3. Once you have added all the answer options, share a link to the survey on the class LMS.

4. Have students access the survey and vote for the tool that they think represents the best option for the project.

TEACHING TIPS

▸ As you or your students introduce an app or tool to the class, have a discussion about its purpose and possible classroom or real-world applications.

▸ We highly recommend that you store recommendations for apps, websites, and other technology tools in a shared Google Doc, on a bulletin board, in a class Symbaloo, or in a shared LMS resource folder.

5. Once all students have voted, display the Dotstorming board on a projector, and the class can discuss the results and analyze the pros and cons of each tool option. Help students identify what they liked and disliked about the tool. Using a pros and cons chart can help drive the conversation.

6. To help students develop in their understanding of the quality of the tools, have them write the pros and cons on their own paper and then share their answers with a small group of students to compile a larger list. From this list, the group will need to come to consensus on their top-three answers to be shared as a large group.

7. After the class has compiled its top answers on a piece of chart paper, give each student two sticky dots to be placed on the chart on his or her top two choices. Discuss as a class the top-two pros to look for and the two cons they need to identify to show a tool is not the right tool for a project.

Connections

You can apply this lesson to different content areas in the following suggested ways.

- **English language arts:** Students can choose the best option from a list of digital tools for recording a demonstration of their reading fluency. After the project's completion, students reflect on the different tools they used.

- **Mathematics:** Students can choose a digital tool from a list you provide to create a video or screencast of them solving an area problem. After they all complete their submissions, the class reflects on which tools proved the most effective and why.

- **Social science:** Students can create digital posters about a U.S. state that they research. Provide a list of digital tools for making these multimedia posters, and have students choose the digital tool that works best for them and the goal of the project. After finishing the posters, the class reflects on the different digital tools used.

- **Science:** Students can create presentations about force and motion, using a digital tool from a list you provide. After the project's completion, students reflect on the pros and cons of the tool options.

- **Art:** Students can edit a photo using a digital tool from a list you provide. After students complete the editing process, the class reflects on the pros and cons of the digital tools on the list.

Wow: Identifying the Right Tool for the Task

This lesson focuses on students selecting digital tools that fit specific project requirements and then choosing the tool that will help them best represent their knowledge. Students use information about project requirements and match the requirements to a tool that will promote successful completion of the project.

Process: Debating About the Best Tool

To complete the following three lesson steps, we recommend you use TouchCast (www.touchcast.com), a smart video production website and app for both Apple and Android devices that allows students to create and share interactive videos. If you prefer, you can adapt this process for use with a variety of other options. Options include but are not limited to Google Slides (www.google.com/slides/about), PowerPoint, and iMovie (www.apple.com/imovie).

1. Using voice and choice, students complete a project from the following Connections section using a digital tool of their choice. Have pairs of students who used different tools on similar projects complete thirty-second duels or debates, highlighting why each student thinks he or she chose the best digital tool. Students can do a duel live in person, or they can prerecord it using TouchCast.

2. In the thirty-second duel, students should highlight why they chose their digital tool, the benefits of using the tool, what else they can use the digital tool for, and so on.

Learning goal:
I can identify and use effective digital tools to meet a given task or problem.

TEACHING TIPS

▶ Have students write a reflection on the *I can* statement for this lesson, demonstrating how they will show that they have proficiency in this area.

▶ While students are working on their projects, have students state what tool they will use, why they selected that specific tool instead of others, and how they will use the tool. This information can be used to partner students. For fun, the teacher could create a tournament bracket.

▶ Allow students to suggest other tools or apps that you did not previously introduce to demonstrate their learning.

3. As an extension, you have the option to have students vote on which student won each debate. If students prerecord a debate in TouchCast, they can include a voting option embedded within the video.

Connections

You can apply this lesson to different content areas in the following suggested ways.

- **English language arts:** Students can choose which digital tool to use to create an advertisement for a book recommendation. Students then reflect on the effectiveness of the tool.

- **Mathematics:** Students can choose a digital tool to use to create a step-by-step instructional video that explains long division, and then they can rate whether they chose an effective tool.

- **Social science:** Students can choose which digital tool to use to create a movie about World War II. Students make their movie and then explain why they chose that tool and reflect on its usefulness.

- **Science:** Students can choose a digital tool to use to create a presentation about different ecosystems. Students create the presentation and then reflect on the pros and cons of that digital tool.

- **Physical education:** Students can track their fitness goals using the digital tool of their choice. Then students reflect on how that digital tool helped them track, analyze, and meet their fitness goals.

Planning and Managing Projects

The lessons in this section focus on giving students the tools to create presentations to show their learning. Students will be able to solve problems and complete tasks in a connected environment using multiple resources. Students are becoming more independent at this stage, with the teacher becoming a facilitator to the process. If something doesn't work, students should be encouraged to try again while working toward the most professional-looking creation they are capable of, mastering the skill of creating digitally designed presentations.

Novice: Planning, Managing, and Sharing Online

Students need the integral skill of collaboration to have success in the 21st century. The purpose of this lesson is for students to begin to understand the power of collaborating in a digital format to solve a problem or share learning. Students will work together to complete an assignment that the teacher outlines. This project allows students opportunities to work with people who might live across the globe as we prepare students for college and careers in a collaborative world.

Process: Managing a Collaborative Space

To complete the following four lesson steps, we recommend you use Padlet (https://padlet.com), a website and an app for both Apple and Android devices used to create collaborative spaces. If you prefer, you can adapt this process for use with a variety of other options. Options include but are not limited to Google Sheets (www.google.com/intl/en_us/sheets /about), Google Sites (https://sites.google.com), and Infogram (https://infogram).

1. Go to the Padlet website or download the Padlet app in the App Store on Apple devices or the Play Store on Android devices, and create a free account.

2. Have students click on New to make a Padlet. Students should read the captions under the icons on the page to determine how to best manage the output and input of information on their page. Using the sidebar options in the program, students can choose a wallpaper and pick a theme. They are also able to open comments on posts.

3. Pose a question or an assignment to your students, and state that they will use Padlet to gather and organize information as they collaborate with other students.

4. Students can share or print the completed Padlet without allowing more comments. They have the option to save it as an image, a PDF, or a spreadsheet under the Share/Export/Embed tab.

Learning goal:
I can share my idea or thought through an online collaborative tool that my teacher has provided.

Connections

You can apply this lesson to different content areas in the following suggested ways.

- **English language arts:** Students choose a story and create and manage a site where other students can discuss the story.

- **Mathematics:** Students generate a mathematics word problem that has multiple ways to be solved. Using a tool of their choice, like Google Sheets, they post the problem and share with other students to solve and explain how they solved the problem.

- **Social science:** Give students an essential question such as, How have Native Americans adapted and changed over time? Students then create and manage a site where collaborators can post their answers to this question, add new questions, and post answers to the new questions. Students create a presentation that will help them to share their learning with others.

- **Science:** Students use any app or website of their choosing showing matter in various phases and collaborate with others to identify and explain each phase.

- **English learners:** Students can create an audio recording of their fluency reading and then record their scores for each reading in a Google Form. Over time, they can create a graph, monitor their fluency, and set goals for improvement.

Operational: Communicating With Collaborative Tools to Solve a Problem

Learning goal:
I can communicate online with my peers on a collaborative tool or project.

Collaborative tools can promote discussion among students. In this lesson, students learn to use tools to create a place to share ideas, have a conversation, and come to a consensus even if they live in different locations around the world. The purpose of this lesson is to help students learn how to work together in a group using online digital tools. Students practice making decisions that will allow them to successfully complete a task the teacher gives.

Process: Communicating Through an Online Messaging Tool

Students find online video messaging tools useful for communicating with each other, with another classroom, or even with an expert in the field. To complete the following five lesson steps, we recommend you use Skype (www.skype.com /en), one such app that includes video and instant messaging. You can install it on any type of digital device. This great technology tool extends communication beyond the classroom. If you prefer, you can adapt this process for use with a variety of other options. Options for communication tools include but are not limited to Google Hangouts (https:// hangouts.google.com), Google+ Communities (https://plus. google.com/communities), and streaming chat options like TodaysMeet (https://todaysmeet.com).

1. Connect with teachers in different classrooms in the same building or district—or around the world— prior to using Skype to make arrangements for your classroom interactions.

2. Have each collaborating teacher set up a Skype account prior to beginning the lesson.

3. Students need to create a plan for their conversation with other classrooms and determine how they will collect and utilize the information based on the lesson objectives set by teachers and students.

4. Students will click on the Skype icon and start a conversation with a group or person that the teacher has set up for them to connect with. The teacher or student can set this connection up by clicking on the Start Conversation button or clicking a contact.

5. Classes should log in to their Skype accounts at the time teachers have arranged for their classes to "meet." One teacher initiates the call by clicking on the contact and then clicking the phone receiver icon in the program on a computer connected to a projector. When another class answers the call, the two classes connect and can see each other on the projector. If smaller groups are working together on a project, there is no need to use the projector.

TEACHING TIPS

▸ Teachers should continuously model what it looks like to collaborate using online tools. This includes responding and reacting to others' posts and working together to solve a problem. Through modeling, we hope to create critical thinkers rather than just consumers of information.

▸ It will be helpful for students to choose topics that could be answered differently with a focus on the region where the Skype participants reside.

TECH TIPS

▸ Make sure when sharing an online tool with your students that you check the sharing settings. For example, determine whether students should have editing rights or only viewing rights.

▸ See https://education .microsoft.com/skype-in -the-classroom/overview for ideas for various types of lessons, virtual field trips, ways to connect, and projects teachers can use with Skype.

Connections

You can apply this lesson to different content areas in the following suggested ways.

- **English language arts:** Students can generate a set of questions to find out more about another culture, climate, ecosystem, or other topic of interest. The students will connect with another classroom to collaborate on gathering information about the topic and create a shared project to present the information.

- **Mathematics:** Using a problem-based learning project, students will plan and manage to solve a problem using the help of another group of students. Students collaborate on solving their problem by sharing ideas, different strategies, and so on.

- **Social science:** Students can research another geographic area and help another group of students research their own location and then create a chart of similarities and differences. They can then plan a group presentation to share their findings.

- **Science:** In groups of two or three, students can create projects on the life cycles of different animals. Students collaborate with another group of students to complete a presentation to share with the class.

- **Art:** Students work together to research different artists and collect their shared research in a presentation tool of their choosing.

Wow: Designing and Collaborating With Others

In this lesson, teachers challenge students to come up with a project or join a global precreated project. Students will determine what online community they will use or join to share ideas to meet the project's learning outcomes. The lesson focuses on students' ability to identify a place where they can collaborate digitally and then use this digital space to have conversations that lead all participants to new or deeper learning outcomes. Students need to learn how to respond to each other online. Students need to practice how to compromise to

Learning goal:
I can collaborate with my peers in an online community that best suits the learning outcomes of a project.

come to a consensus and how to use problem-solving strategies and metacognitive processes to become successful learners, no matter what life path they choose.

Process: Completing a Collaborative Group Project

To complete the following two lesson steps, we recommend you use Projects by Jen (https://projectsbyjen.com). Jen Wagner is a dynamite educator and creator of this website. Each school year, Jen opens different online collaborative projects that teachers can join on their class's behalf. Jen does the organizing for you; you just have to sign up so your students can participate. If you prefer, you can adapt this process for use with a variety of other options. Other options include but are not limited to Kevin Honeycutt's projects (see http://kevinhoneycutt.org).

1. When students find a project on Projects by Jen that interests them or fits with a curricular topic, register for the project.

2. Have the class conduct the project and then post its results on the site. Students can view the results from all participating schools.

Connections

You can apply this lesson to different content areas in the following suggested ways.

- **English language arts:** Students can design a series of interview questions before they collaborate with another class or an expert. The interview can be about any topic of the students' choice. Students can then utilize the information to write a compare-and-contrast essay or a persuasive essay about why someone should visit the other students' place of residence.

- **Mathematics:** The teacher can register the class for Our Really Exciting Online (O.R.E.O) Project (see http://theoppbj.weebly.com), a mathematics-skills-based global project. Students plan and manage the project as they solve mathematics problems with connected classes.

TEACHING TIPS

▸ Continuously model what it looks like to collaborate online. This includes responding and reacting to others' posts and working together to solve a problem. Don't just post your own ideas; stretch students' thinking.

▸ Demonstrate appropriate responses for online collaboration, such as providing constructive criticism, asking questions, properly disagreeing with someone, and more online collaboration tips.

TECH TIPS

▸ It will help the lesson run smoothly if you teach students to check the sharing settings when working in Google Drive. Everyone needs to understand editing or viewing rights, or students will be unable to work collaboratively on the project.

▸ Anytime you provide an opportunity for students to work in an online collaborative tool, make sure that you have access to the shared student document.

- **Social science:** After learning about continents, countries, and cultures, students can participate in Mystery Skype (https://education.microsoft.com /skype-in-the-classroom/mystery-skype) with another class from a different part of the world, asking yes-or-no questions in order to discover the location of the other classroom based on students' knowledge of these social science topics.

- **Science:** The teacher can join Kevin Honeycutt's 100 Years of Innovation Maker Challenge (see http://bit.ly/2ubczz9). Students then follow the directions of the challenge and work collaboratively with students from all over the world to create a Model T car.

- **Art:** Create a digital portfolio of student work in the form of a website, using Google Sites, the website-design program in Google (https://sites.google .com), to showcase their work and get feedback from others. The students will create labels, categories based on art style, and information sections about famous authors.

Finding Data-Driven Solutions

In the real world, students will be asked to find solutions to problems. They will not be expected to guess, but to look at data in ways that will help them to solve the problem and effect change.

The goal of these lessons is to represent data in new ways. Teachers could include the projects in this section in a Genius Hour study (see Kesler, 2013; www.geniushour.com /2013/03/31/genius-hour-ideas). *Genius Hour* refers to time set aside for students to research and learn about whatever interests them. Different opinions exist about who coined this term, but the idea remains consistent that teachers build time into instruction for student voice and choice. Students determine what they would like to learn about. This can focus on a content area or a topic or stay left open to any area of interest. Students will be communicating with other students, teachers, and community members to collaborate on data collection and create a plan for their learning. With the teacher as facilitator, students develop a question that they would like to answer and use critical thinking skills to plan for how they will research it and find a creative way to present the information they learn to their peers as well as any other audience the teacher and students deem acceptable.

Novice: Collecting Data

The goal of this lesson is to expose students to the data-collection process. They will know how to use different tools to gather data that they can analyze. This lesson empowers students as they look for trends in data and develop conclusions that they can act on. After finishing this lesson, students will use the data they collected to complete the operational lesson to use critical-thinking skills to analyze data.

Process: Watching Data in Real Time

To complete the following five lesson steps, we recommend you use Google Forms (www.google.com/intl/en_us/forms /about), Google Docs (http://docs.google.com), and Twitter (https://twitter.com). If you prefer, you can adapt this process for use with a variety of other options. Options include but are not limited to SurveyMonkey (www.surveymonkey.com), Microsoft Word, and Google+ Communities (https://plus .google.com/communities).

1. Have students create surveys in Google Forms to survey their friends about topics they select.

2. Collect links to students' individual forms on a shared Google Doc. Once students have submitted all their forms, you can post the links on the class LMS.

3. Share the classroom website's address with your colleagues, and ask them to have their students take the surveys.

4. Students can watch the data pour in by viewing the response spreadsheet feature in Google Forms (go to the Response tab on the Google Form to see graphs, charts, and summaries of information). Another

Learning goal:
I can collect data using student-created questions via an online response system to investigate trends.

TEACHING TIPS

▸ Analyze data with students.

▸ Help students develop conclusions about the data through class discussions.

view is available under the Google Forms drop-down menu, as Show Summary of Responses.

5. You can share the link, which could be where it is posted on your class website or a direct link on Twitter to reach a broader audience.

Connections

You can apply this lesson to different content areas in the following suggested ways. In each situation, when the data is being entered or answered (if appropriate), the teacher can project the result tool for the students to watch the real-time data results change as new answers are received.

- **English language arts:** First, have the class brainstorm questions that best represent the needed data they want to collect. The topics for questions could be about a book students have read, a piece of poetry, characteristics of a good story, or what genre of writing is most interesting. Then, create a master form, and have students use the form to input daily, weekly, and monthly data. After a period of time, the class investigates together trends in the data and develops conclusions.

- **Mathematics:** While students study data and graphing, have them create their own survey questions. The survey questions could be: What is your favorite TV show? What color car is safest? Who is your favorite superhero and why? Students then put their question and answer choices into an online response system, such as a Google Form, and send the form out to their peers for their response. Other classrooms can use the collected data to create their own graphs based on the results. This can be done by sharing the form with other classes, or allowing them to copy the form and collect and add their own data. They can then share and compare their findings.

- **Social science:** Students can create a survey about an event at school using Google Forms. Students collect the data and create charts and graphs with the results. Examples could include looking for answers to social issues to determine what social issues students in their school might need adults to help with, or surveying to gather data to have their school institute a new policy such as allowing gum in school.

- **Science:** Throughout the year, collect data on the weather in different parts of the world. Have students share observations of weather conditions and investigate the trends that they notice throughout the different months. Students can use anemometers, barometers, thermometers, and wind and rain gauges, or they can just search Google for daily weather readings.

- **Physical education:** Students can use an online data-collection tool to log how many minutes of physical activity they participate in each day.

Operational: Analyzing the Data

In this lesson, teachers have students identify a problem, which can come from previously gathered data from the novice lesson or another data set, or a data set they locate online. Students will then create their own questions and gather data that will help them analyze this additional information to look for trends and themes to deepen their understanding of the topic. After completing the operational lesson, students can use this information to complete the wow lesson to find a solution to the problem they have been analyzing with data.

Process: Designing Data

To complete the following seven lesson steps, we recommend you use data gathered in the previous novice lesson. If your students are advanced enough and do not need to use the novice lesson, you can share the topics with them or have them generate their own ideas for a problem-solving project. For the planning part of the presentation of the analyzed data, use Lucidchart (www.lucidchart.com) to organize the project. Then students will use Lucidpress (www.lucidpress .com), a website where students and teachers can create stunning brochures, fliers, digital magazines, newsletters, and reports. It does not require users to install anything on a device, and users can add all types of media to their project

Learning goal:
I can identify a problem and collect data using student-created questions via an online response system and analyze the collected data.

with a simple drag-and-drop interface. If you prefer, you can adapt this process for use with a variety of other options. Options include but are not limited to Photoshop (www .adobe.com/photoshop), Microsoft Publisher (https://office .microsoft.com/publisher), Google Slides (www.google.com /slides/about), and Adobe Spark (https://spark.adobe.com).

TEACHING TIPS

▸ Lead a class discussion with students on good questions and what types of questions they want to ask so they get valuable data.

▸ Questions for the project should not be questions that students can google for an immediate answer. Students need practice creating good questions.

1. Have students pick a problem to solve and gather data to use in a presentation. Use Connection ideas from the novice lesson, Connection ideas from this lesson, or a problem they might know of that they are passionate about.

2. Students should utilize their data findings to create a process for solving a problem of their choosing and explain how the data they have collected support their plan.

3. While analyzing the data, students should be looking for trends, gaps, or areas of concern that will help them share what they have learned and help them look for a solution to the problem they are trying to solve.

4. Have students sign up for Lucidchart using their Google login. This program will allow students to create a plan that they will then follow to design their brochure in Lucidpress, which is the design program that is a companion to Lucidchart. You could also create a class account for all students to use.

5. Tell students to use the flowchart pictures from Lucidchart and create a visual map of the proposed steps needed to resolve the problem or to move forward with the plan.

6. Students can then download the map they create as a PDF or image file and place it in a document that can be shared in the LMS site so the teacher and other students can give feedback.

7. The students complete the project, using Lucidpress to share their plan, with a written explanation of the process they propose and their reasoning for each step. If desired, the brochures can be shared with

other classes, the school board, and the community to get help in solving the problems the students have chosen to work on for this project.

Connections

You can apply this lesson to different content areas in the following suggested ways.

- **English language arts:** Students can create an online form that they use to track their own reading data, such as fluency or comprehension. Students analyze their own data, find trends and identify a problem in their own progress, and work to eliminate this problem. They will use a tool of their choosing to present their findings to the class, specifically addressing why they selected that tool.

- **Mathematics:** Students can create an online quiz reviewing a mathematics topic or unit of study. They then give the quiz to the class and analyze the results of the questions. The students then find an area of weakness that their class needs to focus on before taking a summative assessment. They will use a tool of their choosing to present to their findings to the class, specifically addressing why they selected that tool.

- **Social science:** Students can identify a problem, such as bullying, in their class, school, or community. Students then generate questions about the problem and create a Google Form with these questions and analyze the resulting answers. For example, if students identify bullying as an issue in their school, they can create an online survey to figure out where, when, and why bullying happens and what consequences the school has for bullying. They then analyze the results to find common trends and themes. They will use a tool of their choosing to present their findings to the class, specifically addressing why they selected that tool.

- **Science:** Students can create an online survey for their community about energy usage, asking questions such as, Do you drive, take public transit, walk, or ride a bike to school or work? Students then analyze the resulting data, finding an area within the data on which the community can improve regarding its energy usage. They will use a tool of their choosing to present their findings to the class, specifically addressing why they selected that tool.

- **Physical education:** Students can create an online survey for their community about healthy eating. Students send the survey out and analyze the resulting data. Students use the data to identify a problem within the community about unhealthy eating habits. They will use a tool of their choosing to present their findings to the class, specifically addressing why they selected that tool.

Wow: Finding the Solution

The goal for this lesson is for students to know how to use data they collected and analyzed to allow them to identify a problem and design a solution. Students can use data from the novice lesson and analyzed data from the operational lesson to complete this assignment. If they were advanced enough to skip those lessons, then they will need to start this lesson by picking a topic, collecting data, and analyzing it to find a solution. This lesson focuses on students using a digital tool to come up with action plans to solve the problem they identify.

Process: Creating an Infographic

Infographics present information quickly and clearly in a visually appealing manner. To complete the following two lesson steps, we recommend you use Piktochart (https://pik tochart.com), a template-driven website for easily creating stunning infographics. It has free and premium features. If you prefer, you can adapt this process for use with a variety of other options. Options include but are not limited to Haiku Deck (www.haikudeck.com), Prezi (https://prezi.com), Google Slides (www.google.com/slides/about), and PowerPoint.

1. If students are advanced enough, they can create an education account on Piktochart, and then click on the media that they want to create. To scaffold learning, the teacher can create the media for some

Learning goal:

I can identify a problem and collect data using student-created questions via an online response system and analyze the collected data to present a possible solution.

or all students to copy and then modify for their use. Options include infographics, presentations, and printable formats.

2. Have students create their own presentations or modify premade teacher presentations using the data they have gathered and analyzed in the Novice and Operational lessons or that they chose to gather for this lesson in order to create their unique infographic for their presentation.

Connections

You can apply this lesson to different content areas in the following suggested ways.

- **English language arts:** Students can create an online survey to analyze how much community members read at home. They gather the data and analyze the trends, and then identify a problem in the data and present a solution of how to encourage more community members to read at home.

- **Mathematics:** Students can design a mathematics problem and send the problem out to the class, the community, or a global audience via an online response system. They then collect data on all the answers and analyze the data to find common misconceptions within the solutions. Finally, have students present the data and develop a lesson in order to provide reteaching that addresses the common misconceptions that occurred.

- **Social science:** Students can create an online survey about economic spending, analyzing what people in their community spend the most money on, such as gas, groceries, utility bills, clothing, and entertainment. Next, they send the survey out to the community and analyze the data, finding a problem in the community's spending, and then create a presentation about spending trends and offer solutions to spending issues within the community.

- **Science:** Students can create an online survey about throwing away trash versus recycling, analyzing the data to figure out how many people recycle

TECH TIPS

▸ We recommend you have students find and save all needed pictures for the infographic in a folder. This will streamline the creation process of the final product.

▸ When students turn in their final infographic, have them share the link to the electronic version in the class LMS to be used for teacher review, sharing with peers, and sharing with global connections.

DISCUSSION QUESTIONS

Consider the following questions for personal reflection or in collaborative work with colleagues.

▸ Why is it important for students to select the digital tools they will use?

▸ What do student voice and choice mean with regard to working with digital tools?

▸ What is an infographic, and which technology tools could you use to create one?

▸ What are three collaborative tools from this chapter that interest you? Write a few sentences about each one.

▸ What is an example of a video-messaging system, and how could you use this in your classroom?

▸ What is one new technology tool you learned about in this chapter, and how do you plan on using it in your classroom?

▸ Which lesson idea from this chapter will you try in your classroom, and why?

▸ What is one resource from this chapter you will share with your colleagues, and why?

▸ What is one way you can connect to the curriculum for students working with data?

and how their community can do a better job of recycling materials. They then present the data to the community and propose possible solutions to improve recycling in the community and limit unnecessary waste.

- **Physical education:** Students can create an online survey about how much physical activity people participate in each day, sending the survey out to all members of the school—both adults and students. Students analyze the data, identify a problem within the data, and create a presentation about the strengths and weaknesses of the school community's healthy lifestyle and possible solutions for the weaknesses.

Conclusion

Student voice and choice meet data decisions in this chapter. We know change will remain the only constant in students' future, and our students need to become digital explorers who can try different tools and compare and contrast their features. Selecting the best technology tool for a task takes critical thinking, trial and error, practice, and problem-solving skills. Students get practice in working in collaborative teams to come to consensus to solve real-world problems. Students need to have a variety of experiences using different technology tools to know how to describe why one tool better serves a purpose than another.

For some readers, the tools and activities this chapter featured may appear new and unfamiliar, but we believe when you have tried one of this chapter's lessons, such as creating infographics using data sets, the beautiful products students create will surprise you. Every lesson in this chapter incorporated the four Cs, further developing the future-ready skills for teachers and students.

Being Responsible Digital Citizens

Digital citizens must recognize the responsibilities and opportunities to learn and interact with others in a digital environment. According to the ISTE (2016) standards, students need to learn how to be responsible online, protect their digital identity, and behave ethically while using digital resources. We believe developing digital citizens should not be isolated and taught in one lesson; instead, the concepts in this chapter should be part of daily lessons.

According to Mary Beth Hertz (2015), "With children spending time online at younger and younger ages, it is vital that we explicitly teach young children how to protect themselves online." Students in the 21st century classroom are digital citizens. They know how to navigate the Internet and quickly obtain information, but do they think about staying safe when they go online?

Footprints in the sand easily get washed away; unfortunately, we cannot easily delete our digital footprints. Teachers need to inform students well of the pros and cons of using all forms of online resources so that they know how to leave a positive digital footprint. Dictionary.com defines a *digital footprint* as "one's unique set of digital activities, actions, and communications that leave a data trace on the Internet or on a computer or other digital device" (Digital footprint, n.d.). Educators can use the lessons in this chapter to prepare students for the goal of college and career readiness while they stay safe and maintain a positive digital footprint. Through these lessons, students will learn how to keep themselves and their personal information safe online. Students will also understand the importance of creating original work and citing the sources they use in their projects. For information about the tools we mention in these lessons, and for clarity on technology terms you may encounter in this chapter, see the appendix on page 133. Visit **go.SolutionTree .com/technology** to download a free reproducible version of this appendix and to access live links to the tools mentioned in this book.

Teachers can pick and choose the lessons they find appropriate for their students. The timing of the lessons can correspond to and integrate into any subject-area lesson for greatest effectiveness and for maximizing student understanding of the following important topics: ensuring Internet safety, understanding legal and ethical behaviors, and managing one's digital footprint.

Ensuring Internet Safety

In this section, students will identify the components of Internet safety and digital citizenship through class discussion and interaction with Internet safety sites that give information as well as provide simulations for students to learn through trial-and-error activities. It will be important that students do more than just learn the components; they need to become effective in their use to stay safe online.

Novice: Identifying Internet Safety Components

The purpose of this lesson is to help students understand the importance of Internet safety and identify its components. With 21st century learners, Internet safety needs to be a top priority, as students can access the Internet from school and home. Just as we make teaching our students about real-world *stranger danger* a priority, stranger danger also applies to the virtual world of the Internet. Student safety online should be a top concern for all of us as educators.

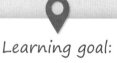

Learning goal:
I can identify the components of Internet safety (including cyberbullying, passwords, and privacy and knowing when to click on something, download something, and ask for help).

Process: Understanding Internet Safety

Common Sense Media (www.commonsensemedia.org) is an independent nonprofit website focused on media use and children. It has designed the program Digital Passport (www .digitalpassport.org) to teach digital citizenship. Use Digital Passport to complete the following six steps for this lesson. If you prefer, you can adapt this process for use with a variety of other options. One additional option for Internet safety is NetSmartz (www.netsmartz.org), a website with resources a teacher can use to support digital citizenship education in the classroom.

1. The teacher creates an educator account in Digital Passport (www.digitalpassport.org/educator -registration) and completes the registration process.

2. Next, he or she creates a group in Digital Passport and enters the students' names.

3. Then, the teacher customizes the activities of the group to align with the lesson objectives of identifying the following Internet safety components.

   - Addressing cyberbullying

   - Creating passwords and privacy

   - Knowing when to click on something, to download something

   - Asking for help

4. Students join the group by entering the class code the website generates.

5. Students earn badges as they work through the modules.

6. The teacher uses the reports page in Digital Passport to view the work of individuals and the group.

Connections

You can apply this lesson to different content areas in the following suggested ways.

- **English language arts:** After reading a read-aloud book about bullying, lead a class discussion to specifically focus on the topic of *cyberbullying*. Look at examples, discuss steps to take if students

TEACHING TIPS

▸ Whenever possible, use current events to bring the topic of digital citizenship into the classroom discussion about online safety.

▸ Don't overdo the stranger danger approach to learning and collaborating online. Students need to be aware but not made to be fearful enough to be unwilling to use the Internet. The Internet is part of our students' daily lives, and as educators, it is our job to help keep them safe online.

TECH TIPS

▸ For any projects or visual representations created, make sure students share with the teacher, through the class LMS, the project or link to the website where they are creating their work.

▸ Teachers may want to create a shared Google Doc or file on the LMS with links to research sites or articles to guide novice students in their research.

come across a cyberbully, and discuss knowing when to ask for help. As a class, generate a poster for the classroom.

- **Mathematics:** Discuss different ways advertisers use spam and place links on websites, like in sidebars and pop-ups, and describe how spam and pop-ups may link to other appropriate or inappropriate websites. Students should always consult an adult with any questions related to staying safe online. Have groups of students research the extent of the online spam problem and create visual representations of the numerical data they discover.

- **Social science:** Discuss with students that there are always many users online, both those we know and those we don't. Address what students can appropriately share with users online and cannot. Inform students that they should always ask for help if they feel unsure about a certain situation. Our students have access to almost unlimited data, but historically, information was not always shared openly online like it is today. Let groups of students research times in history when information was limited, or when the slow delivery of information impacted an outcome (for example, Paul Revere's ride, explorers' new discoveries, and so on).

- **Science:** Have small groups research the career of a data scientist and create infographics including information about what students should and should not share online. Discuss what information students can share online (for example, just their first names) and what students should *not* share, including their addresses, phone numbers, and passwords. Discuss which websites students need parental permission to use and why they need to protect themselves. Finish the lesson by talking about how changing digital citizenship needs is creating new career opportunities like data scientists.

Operational: Explaining How to Stay Safe Online

The purpose of this lesson is to enable students to explain the importance of Internet safety. Students should take what they have learned about Internet safety and apply it in order to explain why they personally find it important. When students can explain why it has importance, they will more likely know how to exhibit safe Internet behaviors at school and at home.

Process: Using Digital Citizenship Sites to Explain Information About Internet Safety

Groups of students will create a digital presentation about one of the following Internet safety topics: addressing cyberbullying, creating passwords and protecting privacy, knowing when to click on or to download something, and asking for help. These presentations will be shared with younger students in grades K–2.

This lesson will focus on the art of sketchnoting to visually represent ideas. *Sketchnoting* is the process of combining words and images to help remember key ideas like the Internet safety tips your students will be teaching the younger students. Most sketchnotes are done using paper, pencil, and markers. However, for this lesson, each group will select how it would like to create the presentation using digital tools, allowing for creativity and student voice and choice. To complete the following six lesson steps, we recommend you use a drawing app such as Google Drawings, (https://drawings.google.com), Educreations (www.educreations.com), or Explain Everything (https://explaineverything.com).

1. Without using Google, have students brainstorm what they think the term *sketchnoting* means.

2. Show students the YouTube video at http://bit.ly/2uFN5M3 to introduce sketchnoting to the entire class.

3. Compare students' responses to the brainstorm from step 1 to the information in the video, and have students do a practice sketchnote.

Learning goal:
I can explain why each component of Internet safety (including cyberbullying, passwords, and privacy and knowing when to click on something, download something, and ask for help) is important.

TEACHING TIPS

▸ Sketchnoting can be done with digital tools or using paper and pencil. This fresh twist on doodling can help students make connections between ideas in different lessons within the chapter.

▸ Not everyone will be comfortable sketchnoting; make sure students have options.

TECH TIPS

▸ Paper and pencil works for sketchnoting, but so do many apps, extensions, and digital programs.

▸ Students can use a variety of styluses with a tablet or a touch screen.

4. In small groups, have students select an Internet safety topic and create a rough draft sketchnote based on the topic.

5. After discussing the sketchnote plan, students will use an Apple or Android drawing app such as Google Drawings, Educreations, or Explain Everything to create their first sketchnote.

6. When completed, students can share the sketchnotes with the teacher and also with younger K–2 students through the LMS.

Connections

You can apply this lesson to different content areas in the following suggested ways.

- **English language arts:** While teaching K–2 students about cyberbullying, your students can practice their speaking and listening skills. Students can explain what cyberbullying involves and provide examples with steps on how to solve cyberbullying problems.

- **Mathematics:** Have groups of students use the website Internet Web Stats (www.internetlivestats .com) to research the numbers of social media users and create a digital presentation about keeping personal information private online. Take just one part of the data, and represent it in a digital presentation.

- **Social science:** Have students research Morse code and why this language was created. Compare and contrast that to students today communicating with unknown users online.

Wow: Showing How to Stay Safe Online

The purpose of this lesson is to allow students to demonstrate the importance of online safety and how it directly relates to their personal Internet usage outside of school. Many times, Internet safety gets overlooked because students and adults alike feel as though it does not pertain to them. However, Internet safety pertains to everyone, everyday, everywhere.

Learning goal:

I can demonstrate how to exercise each component of Internet safety in my daily Internet usage at home and at school.

Process: Conducting an Internet Safety Audit

Internet safety and practicing digital citizenship should not end when the bus pulls away from school at the end of the day. Students need to help educate and protect their families when they are using digital devices at home. The assignment for students is to create an Internet safety audit for family members. First, students will assess each family member's level of Internet safety knowledge. The topics to focus on include the following Internet safety elements: addressing cyberbullying, creating passwords and protecting privacy, knowing when to click on or download something, and asking for help. After the results are received, the student will lead a family discussion, recording notes in the spreadsheet of results. The student will record notes, questions, and concerns about what they teach their families. To complete the following five lesson steps, we recommend you use Google Forms (www.google.com/intl/en_us/forms/about). If you prefer, you can adapt this process for use with a variety of other options. Other options include but are not limited to Survey Monkey (www.surveymonkey.com) or similar online survey sites.

1. Each student creates a Google Form to survey his or her family about the Internet safety topics of addressing cyberbullying, creating passwords and protecting privacy, knowing when to click on or download something, and asking for help.

2. The students share the survey link with their family members and ask everyone to complete the form.

3. Once the survey results are returned, the students analyze the results, making notes in the spreadsheet created from the original Google Form.

4. The students discusses the results with their families and share what they have learned about Internet safety.

5. The students summarize the results in the spreadsheet and share the spreadsheet with the teacher through the classroom LMS.

Connections

You can apply this lesson to different content areas in the following suggested ways.

TEACHING TIPS

▸ Creating anchor charts of safety tips to place around the room will help students remember important tips while they are using digital tools.

▸ After the students teach their families, help them look for themes and similarities as groups, and talk about next steps.

- **English language arts:** Students create a public service announcement about cyberbullying to fulfill speaking and listening learning goals. This project should include a definition of *cyberbullying*, how to stop this problem behavior, how to deal with a cyberbully, and when to ask a trusted adult for help.

- **Mathematics:** Students can create an infographic to inform peers about who they consider trusted adults online. Topic examples include stranger danger and good strangers versus bad strangers. Learn about the tools students can use to create infographics in chapter 4 (page 71).

- **Social science:** In many homes today, children know more about technology than their parents. Is this similar to any other time in history? Students will compare and contrast understanding technology to learning a new language before their parents or grandparents.

- **Music:** Students can create a rap about what personal information students should keep private. Students can use AutoRap (http://apple.co/1h1EEqL), an app available on both Apple and Android devices.

Understanding Legal and Ethical Behaviors

Just because information is available on the Internet doesn't mean you can take someone else's work and put your name on it. Students need to understand the legal and ethical behaviors of learning and working in a digital environment. Citing sources on a page, creating a list of sources in a project, and formally citing sources are progressive skills that are very important for students to apply.

Novice: Citing Sources on a Page

This lesson introduces students to the importance of giving credit to sources when they use a source's words or pictures in their work. Students need to include a source's name on the page that contains information or graphics from that source. This lesson prepares students to develop a set of skills needed

Learning goal:
I can give credit for words and pictures by putting the source's name on the page on which they appear.

to formally cite sources, which students need throughout school and their future careers.

Process: Writing a Digital Postcard to a Friend

In this lesson, students will create informational postcards. To complete the following five lesson steps, we recommend you use Adobe Spark (http://spark.adobe.com), a template-driven website for designing brochures, postcards, invitations, and posters. It has free and premium templates to select from to create a final product. If you prefer, you can adapt this process for use with a variety of other options. Options include but are not limited to Google Slides (www.google.com/slides /about), Lucidpress (www.lucidpress.com), and Canva (www .canva.com).

1. Students should navigate to Adobe Spark (https://spark.adobe.com) and sign in with their Google account.

2. Have students create a page instead of a post or video.

3. Students add a title and a subtitle.

4. Next, students click on the plus sign to add the research summary paragraph.

5. Students cite the source of the information by adding the web address of where they found the information and the picture.

Connections

You can apply this lesson to different content areas in the following suggested ways.

- **English language arts:** During a novel study, have groups of students collect pictures about the setting of the book. Groups should cite each picture by copying the website address and pasting it below the picture. Also, have the groups write a caption about why they selected each image, connecting back to the book.

- **Mathematics:** Students can learn about a mathematician. Have students create a Google Slides presentation highlighting events in the mathematician's life and add pictures. Below each

TEACHING TIPS

▸ Show students published work that includes citations. Have students discuss why the publications might include these citations.

▸ Ask your school librarian (the information specialist in the building) to help with this lesson.

TECH TIPS

▸ Copying and pasting a website address might be a new skill for some students. Make sure they copy the entire address to connect back to the original source.

▸ On Adobe Spark, students can download the image by clicking on the Share button, copying the link, and posting the link to the classroom LMS.

picture, students copy and paste the web address of the resource.

- **Social science:** Have students search online to find the population and socioeconomics of a community they are studying, including race, age distribution, household income, and education level, and then cite the source where the information was found by copying and pasting the web address.

- **Science:** Students create an infographic highlighting a chemical element from the periodic table, including informative pictures and text. Below each picture, students copy and paste the web address that the picture came from.

- **Art:** Students can create a collage of pictures to represent an art style. Below each picture, students insert the name of the picture's source.

Operational: Creating a List of Sources

This lesson prompts students to make a list of the sources that they use throughout a project and then list those sources at the end of their project using web addresses or shortened URLs. Many addresses can be very long and distract from the student work, so by shortening the URLs, projects look neater, but the reader can still access the source. Students need to develop the necessary skills of giving credit when needed and formally citing all sources in a bibliography at the end of a project when they use websites, books, or other sources to support their work. Students will continue to develop these skills and use them throughout their school career and life.

Process: Citing Sources With Shortened Web Addresses

Websites often have long addresses—or *URLs* (uniform resource locators). Every webpage has its own unique address, and as pages are added to websites, the addresses tend to become longer. To complete the following steps, we recommend you use Google URL Shortener (https://goo.gl). If you prefer, you can adapt this process for use with a variety of other options. Options include but are not limited to Bitly (https://bitly.com) and TinyURL (https://tinyurl.com).

Learning goal:

I can give credit for others' work by posting a list of credits at the end of my project.

1. Students should each create a Google Doc titled "How and Why to Shorten a Web Address." As they learn about how to shorten a web address, they will be creating a how-to guide they will share with another student in another class.

2. Students go to a website like Google Earth (www .google.com/earth) and copy the web address to their clipboard. The first step is to highlight the URL and select Copy from the Edit menu. The keyboard shortcut to do this is Command or Control + C.

3. Next, the student opens the Google URL Shortener (https://goo.gl) and pastes the web address into the first box in the form.

4. After that, the student selects Shorten URL and then copies the new shortened web address that the site generates.

5. Students return to the Google Doc they created and paste the new shortened address into the document.

6. Students write the steps to shorten a URL in their document and share the Google Doc with someone in another classroom, using the sharing settings.

Connections

You can apply this lesson to different content areas in the following suggested ways.

- **English language arts:** Students can create a research paper about a famous novel. On a separate page, students create a bibliography, listing all the sites, books, and resources they used in the research paper using the shortened URLs.

- **Mathematics:** Students learn how to use a mathematics concept in the real world and create a slide show demonstrating their learning. The last slide features a bibliography, listing all the shortened website addresses, books, and other resources they used to create the slideshow.

- **Social science:** Students can research a landform and create a stop-motion video showing how the landform evolved over years. The last frames of the stop-motion video display a list of all the websites, books, and other resources they used to create the video.

- **Science:** Students work with a lab partner to research a topic. The group lists the websites they used to gather information, using shortened URLs.

- **Art:** Students can create a slide show highlighting the works of an artist. The last slide displays a list of all the websites, books, and other resources they used to create the slide show.

Wow: Creating Hyperdocs

In this lesson, students will learn how to create a hyperdoc with embedded web addresses to cite where they found their information. A *hyperdoc* is any online document with links to other resources. In a hyperdoc, the links are often "hidden" behind a keyword. This lesson will teach students how to "hide" the website addresses to make a document more visually appealing. Many websites conceal links this way, including Wikipedia (https://en.wikipedia.org). Teachers must teach this lesson to students of all ages because students need to give credit to sources they cite before they post any work on online sources, such as YouTube or blogs. Previous lessons in this chapter helped students determine when they need to give credit, and in this lesson, educators teach students how to give credit correctly. To complete the following six lesson steps, we recommend you use Google Docs (https://docs.google.com). If you prefer, you can adapt this process for use with a variety of other options. Other options include but are not limited to Microsoft Word and Microsoft PowerPoint.

Process: Giving Credit Correctly

Wikipedia provides good examples of what a hyperdoc looks like, so in this lesson, students will be creating their own hyperdoc about something they are studying using resources from Wikipedia.

1. Groups of students discuss what they know about the website Wikipedia.

2. One member of the group creates a Google Doc and shares it with the teacher and other group members.

Learning goal:

I can create a hyperdoc with embedded web addresses to cite where I found my information.

3. The group researches and records what it learns in the shared Google Doc. To turn this Google Doc into a hyperdoc, the links to the research websites are embedded into the document.

4. Once the group has a paragraph of text, students are ready to add the websites they want to cite. To do this, they copy the website address, and in their paragraph, they highlight a key word in the document connected to the research. This key word is the word students will hyperlink to the original cited source.

5. Next, from the Insert menu, students select Link. They paste the website link into the form, and now the word in their paragraph is highlighted to indicate the reader can click on that word to go to the website.

6. The group cites at least three resources to complete their hyperdoc.

Connections

You can apply this lesson to different content areas in the following suggested ways.

- **English language arts:** Students can read a novel that has been made into a movie. They then do research and develop a presentation that compares and contrasts the movie and book versions. Students use the presentation tool that they determine will best communicate the information, and they will embed the links into the presentation.

- **Mathematics:** Students can research how a mathematical formula got developed and choose a presentation tool to communicate this information. Students will embed the links into the presentation.

- **Social science:** Students can research a country and choose the presentation tool that will best communicate the information they find. Students will embed the links into the presentation.

- **Science:** Students can research a scientific testing procedure and choose the tool that will best

TEACHING TIPS

- ▸ Once students know how to create a hyperdoc, they should use this format whenever possible to make documents look more uniform.

- ▸ Now that students know how to create a hyperdoc, encourage them to teach a student in another class how to do this.

TECH TIPS

- ▸ Once a student clicks on the embedded hyperlink, the color of the link usually changes.

- ▸ Hyperdocs can also be created in word processing programs like Microsoft Word and in presentation programs like Microsoft PowerPoint and Google Slides.

communicate the information they find. Students will embed the links into the presentation.

- **Art:** Students can research an art form and choose the presentation tool that will best communicate the information they find. Students will embed the links into the presentation.

Managing One's Digital Footprint

A digital footprint is a collection of all the things that you have posted online. It is extremely important to teach students that anything they post online stays online. The powerful tool of the Internet can have a huge positive impact; for example, students can raise awareness of a disease, raise money for a family in need, or celebrate successes on the Internet. However, you must note to students that all things they post have the ability to reach a large audience, and once they make posts, they can never really fully delete them.

Novice: Explaining Why I Need to Protect Information Online

This lesson focuses on protecting personal information online. Teachers need to help students recognize and explain why they should not share personal information online. Students will learn what information they should not post in any online forum, such as their full name, address, and phone number. Students can use the Internet as a wonderful place to share, learn, and explore, but students need to do so in a safe manner.

Process: Learning About Digital Footprints

To complete the following seven lesson steps, we recommend you use Safe Search Kids (www.safesearchkids.com), a free search engine for students. If you prefer, you can adapt this process for use with a variety of other options. Other options include but are not limited to Kidtopia (www.kidtopia.info) and Infotopia (www.infotopia.info).

1. Each search engine indexes information in a different way, so students should practice using a

Learning goal:
I can explain why I need to protect my personal information online.

variety of search engines to begin to understand how information is organized online. Have students use Safe Search Kids to practice using search engines other than Google and to collect information about digital footprints.

2. Groups of students will work together to research what a digital footprint is. One member of the group creates a Google Doc and shares it with editing rights. Next, he or she shares the Google Doc with the team and the teacher. The team members conduct research and record their findings in the document.

3. Before going online, the group should brainstorm what search terms they will use, and what information they think they will find. This should be recorded in the Google Doc.

4. Groups of students should discuss what they learned and summarize the discussion by creating a list of keywords to remember about a digital footprint.

5. Next, students copy the list of words and navigate to the tag cloud generator Word Art (https://wordart.com).

6. Students then manipulate how big the keywords are on the Word Art website by adjusting the size in the word section. The groups should decide which words should be larger or more prominent in the final picture.

7. These images could be posted around the school to help other students learn about their digital footprint.

Connections

- **English language arts:** Have students select a character from a book, and have them make up ten search results about that character that would show what the character's digital footprint might look like.

- **Mathematics:** Have students work in partners to search for the keywords they searched for in

TEACHING TIPS

▶ The teacher should lead a class discussion about what students should never share online, including the following pieces of private information: full name, address, town, phone number, age, birth date, and school name. Additional pieces of information will vary based on the class.

▶ Talking about students' digital footprints should not be isolated to one or two lessons. Whenever possible, use current events to talk about Internet safety.

▶ Comparing research of different search engines will help students better understand how information is organized.

TECH TIPS

▶ Word clouds use text to emphasize word frequency in writing. When using an online word cloud generator for a class project, practice how to make individual words larger with students ahead of time.

▶ Using the advanced search in Google, students can refine searches and look for more specific information to help them in their projects.

the lesson. In Google Sheets, have the students record how many results they received when they searched in two different search engines and discuss why the number of results is not the same in each search engine.

- **Social science:** The teacher should lead a discussion about primary-source documents and how these documents serve as a type of footprint. Good examples can be found at the Library of Congress website—specifically in the collections section (www.loc.gov/collections).

- **Science:** Have groups of students search for infographics about digital footprints. Each group should copy the infographics and place them each on a Google Slide. Compare and contrast the information, and look at the sources and dates of the infographics. The groups can record their thoughts in the speaker notes in Google Slides and submit the presentation using the class LMS.

Operational: Creating a Positive Online Image

Learning goal:

I can explain when and where I should make posts and how they reflect my online image.

This lesson focuses on teaching students when and where they should make posts online and how their posts reflect their online image. Students will make posts online using a variety of social media outlets regardless of whether their classroom covers them. We need to teach students how to make posts in a respectful and positive manner. This lesson shows students how people can interpret messages in different ways online and teaches them about appropriate places to make posts. Students need to recognize that they can use social media in very positive ways and it can have a huge impact on their lives.

Process: Practicing Positive Online Behaviors

To complete the following four lesson steps, we recommend you use TodaysMeet (https://todaysmeet.com), a website for creating free online collaborative spaces (referred to as *rooms*) to communicate with students. If you prefer, you can adapt this process for use with a variety of other options. Other options include but are not limited to Padlet (https://padlet.com) or a shared Google Doc.

1. The teacher creates a free TodaysMeet account and then creates an online space. Select how long you will keep the room active. We suggest keeping the room for a year.

2. Have students access the room by sharing the link to the room on the class LMS. Students type in just their first names, and then they can start to collaborate with other students in the class by typing a message and pressing the Say button.

3. The teacher types questions about Internet safety and digital footprints for students to respond to in the room.

4. Project the chat so that students can see comments in real time and spark discussion. After each question, the teacher leads a discussion about what makes a good response and what can be improved.

Connections

- **English language arts:** Have students create their own posts on index cards. After they write their posts, students can read other students' posts out loud in different tones of voice (for example, they can read, "Wow, that's cool," in an excited voice, a sarcastic voice, or a monotone voice). Discuss how a post changes when read in different ways and how this reflects on the original intent of the post and the person who wrote it. Students can then comment out loud on each post, and the original writer can say how these comments make him or her feel. End the lesson by discussing when it is appropriate to make a post and how what you post can influence what others think of you.

- **Social science:** Divide the class into teams and have them debate something from history. First have them collaborate and craft their approach to the debate. Next, let the team leader post the group's comments into the room the teacher created on TodaysMeet. Continue the debate about the topic,

> **TEACHING TIPS**
>
> ▶ Use current event opportunities to discuss appropriate commenting on social media.
>
> ▶ When students begin to comment online on a LMS or other website, they will need guidance to stay focused on the topic. Students need to practice online commenting because this will be a big part of their future in the classroom and also in college and careers.

collaborating as needed. Summarize the lesson by reflecting on the tone of the posts.

- **Science:** Use the room the teacher created in TodaysMeet as a question-and-answer forum during a project. After the lesson, the teacher reflects with the students about what questions and answers were helpful.

- **Music:** Use TodaysMeet to create a music room for the school. The teacher plays the role of the famous musician, and the students ask questions about the musician's work and career. The teacher should add a few incorrect answers that students have to research and provide evidence about whether the comment was fact or fiction.

Wow: Explaining How My Digital Footprint Is Important

Learning goal:
I can explain what a digital footprint is and how this is important to me.

The purpose of this lesson is for students to share what they have learned about digital footprints with other students, teachers, and parents in a creative way. Students will be creating short video public service announcements (PSAs) explaining what a digital footprint is and why it is important to them personally.

Process: Creating a Public Service Announcement to Inform Peers

Students will create public service announcement videos that are about thirty seconds long, specifically focusing on why their digital footprint is important to them. The message should be personal yet creative, and that takes planning. Crafting the message and storyboarding the PSA should be done before students touch technology. Students should spend more time planning to help streamline the actual video creation. A quick way to create a storyboard is to have students fold paper into squares. These don't need to be fancy, but they do need to tell a compelling direct message. To complete the following eight lesson steps, we recommend you use WeVideo (www.wevideo.com), which can be used on any device. If you prefer, you can adapt this process for use with a variety of other options. Other options include but are not limited to iMovie (www.apple.com/imovie) or the website Animoto (https://animoto.com).

1. Students will create their own personal message to explain why their digital footprint is important to them. The first step is to define the message.

2. Students should use paper to plan out the PSA message and the sequence of the video they plan on creating.

3. The teacher should approve the storyboard.

4. Next, students should plan how they will produce their videos, including what props and setting they need.

5. Students might need to help each other in the filming process. Once the video is filmed, the students then upload the video clips to their Google Drives.

6. Students open WeVideo as an add-on through their Google Drives, and import their video clips.

7. Students use the editing features to create PSAs that are about thirty seconds long. In WeVideo, students should also include a title and credits at the end if someone helped with the production.

8. Once completed, the final videos are saved to the students' Google Drives and shared with the teacher using the class LMS.

Connections

- **English language arts:** Public service announcements are a great way to practice speaking and listening skills as well as help students understand how media can persuade people with strong messaging.

- **Mathematics:** The entire collection of *Schoolhouse Rock!* videos can be found on the YouTube channel SchoolhouseRockTV1 (www.youtube.com/user /SchoolhouseRockTV1). Groups of students should compare and contrast how two of the mathematics videos were created.

TEACHING TIPS

- Tweet about a class activity, and study the Twitter analytics (or activity) with the class at the end of the day and again throughout the week, looking at how many people saw or engaged with the tweet, and how its activity changes. Discuss how anything you post can reach many people and how a post becomes a permanent part of your digital footprint, even if you delete it.

- Encourage students to practice with a partner before recording their project to help them practice speaking clearly and at a pace that is understandable to others.

- **Social science:** Students create PSAs as they study about propaganda. Groups should study some examples of posters from World War II to discuss the different messaging. A good lesson is found on the Library of Congress website (https://memory.loc.gov/ammem/awhhtml/awpnp6/worldwars.html).

- **Science:** Have groups of students watch videos on Bill Nye's YouTube channel (www.youtube.com/user/TheRealBillNye/videos). You can then lead a discussion about the techniques used to engage students with science.

Conclusion

In this chapter, we tackled some challenging issues around the topics of Internet safety and security and digital footprints that all students need to understand. We need to help students understand how to create and maintain a positive digital footprint and ensure these lessons stay with students as they start using social media outside of school. Equally important, we must teach students to identify cyberbullying and understand how to interact respectfully with others online. Students must also respect others' intellectual property and know when and how to give credit for online resources that become part of new work products they create. We cannot predict the Internet of the future, but continuous talk about online safety and respect will help our students become positive digital citizens.

Expanding Technology and Coding Concepts

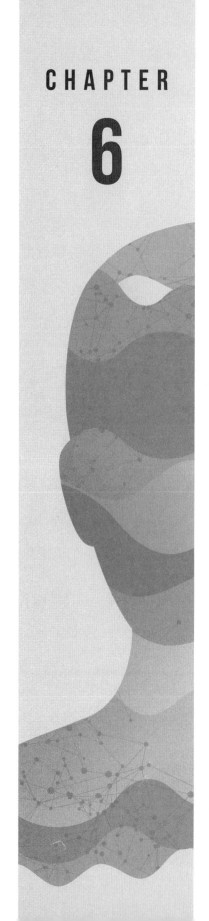

Students in the 21st century classroom come excited and ready to use technology. Lessons in this chapter focus on foundational knowledge of technology operations and concepts—from developing students' understanding of the basic operational uses of devices to introducing them to the intriguing behind-the-scenes world of coding. Teachers can use these lessons to help students become familiar with the inner workings of devices so they can troubleshoot problems, understand the importance of organizing work, and learn a coding language to create a product. For information about the tools we mention in these lessons, and for clarity on technology terms you may encounter in this chapter, see the appendix on page 133. Visit **go.SolutionTree.com/technology** to download a free reproducible version of this appendix and to access live links to the tools mentioned in this book.

In her article "Digital Native vs Digital Citizen?: Examining a Dangerous Stereotype," Mary Beth Hertz (2012) states:

> It's one thing to use a tablet computer and its apps to learn basic literacy skills; but learning to create, read critically, use online content responsibly and be a respectful digital citizen are not always skills that can be learned without the guidance of a teacher.

The role teachers play is more important than ever as we teach our students to become critical thinkers and problem solvers no matter what device they have in front of them in the future. The ISTE (2016) standards challenge teachers to empower the learner and develop computational thinkers and innovative designers. Through customizing their learning environments, helping them understand the fundamental concepts of technology operations, transferring their knowledge to emerging technologies, and utilizing a variety of challenges including coding, we are cultivating these skills and preparing our learners to be ready for any opportunity presented to them in the future. With change as the only constant in the future, our students need to be familiar with and fluent in the topics covered in this chapter: understanding and troubleshooting basic operations; storing, sharing, and managing online files; and coding.

Understanding and Troubleshooting Basic Operations

Teachers will have students work individually when it comes to problem solving and troubleshooting a device. Students need to understand that devices may not work properly all the time and they need to be comfortable navigating ways to troubleshoot them.

Novice: Operating the Device

The goal of this lesson is to have students become proficient in using a device. To complete the following four lesson steps, use electronic devices students routinely have access to in the classroom.

Process: Becoming Familiar With a Device

Lead a class discussion to help students understand the operations of the device. Have students choose and scan articles from two different domains. The students should identify which article contains the needed information based on the facts or opinions stated in the articles and use the best article or articles for their research.

Learning goal:
I can use the basic operations of my device (start it, open apps, go to websites, save, and shut down).

1. The teacher should lead the class in brainstorming about the basic device operations and limitations.

2. Students should work with a partner to compile a list of the operations. After students discuss with a partner, the teacher will compile a list of items from all students.

3. With a list of operations, assign each student one operation to explain in a thirty-second-long video or written how-to guide.

4. Publish these guides on a class website or the library in your LMS, allowing students to access them at any time.

Connections

You can apply this lesson to different content areas in the following suggested ways.

- **English language arts:** Prior to having students begin a project, review procedures for starting up the device they will use, opening needed documents, saving documents, and logging off and shutting down the device.

- **Social science:** Have small groups of students research the history of computers and create a timeline of significant technology-related events in history.

- **Science:** Have groups of students research malware and computer viruses. Have groups compare and contrast how computer viruses are similar to the spread of human diseases.

Operational: Utilizing Shortcuts

The goal of this lesson is to create learners who can use shortcuts to increase their productivity. These shortcuts are simpler ways that allow the student to use the device to its fullest potential. Knowing these shortcuts will also enable students to be more productive as they know how to navigate the device fluently. This lesson focuses on students spending more time on the curriculum and less time on the operations of their device or program. Many shortcuts are universal, and students can use them with any program or platform. This

---

TEACHING TIPS

▸ Working with colleagues and attending professional development sessions help the teachers in a school building understand the features of new technology devices. Great resources include online videos and district technology staff, but don't forget to let students become the experts.

▸ Give groups of students the opportunity to explore the device and teach the rest of the class what they learn.

TECH TIPS

▸ Identify students who are experts with their devices. When certain issues arise, these students can be the go-to people for the class.

▸ Create a group of student helpers based on who feels most comfortable teaching others. Many school districts are creating tech clubs for interested students.

Learning goal:
I can use shortcuts to use my device more effectively.

continuity allows students to become versatile in their ability to pick the best tool for the job they need to complete.

Process: Searching for Shortcuts

In this lesson, students use their research skills to discover ways that they can use their device to its fullest potential. To complete the following four lesson steps, students will need to navigate to a web browser and open up a search engine (we recommend Google). Students will need to keep track of their research by using a word processing tool such as Microsoft Word or Google Docs.

1. To find the most current shortcuts available, have students conduct an online search to identify any available solutions. Students can conduct Google searches for needed shortcuts, such as those to save, print, cut, copy, and paste.

2. Have groups of students research the shortcuts, and let them have voice and choice in how they share this information with the class. These shortcuts will differ from PC to Mac and among the variety of tablets on the market. Students should research the shortcuts for their particular device as a way to learn more about its functions.

3. Have students open a document in Google Docs (https://docs.google.com) or another word processing program and work with a partner to practice the shortcuts.

4. Challenge students to a competition focused on the shortcuts they researched. Have them time each other to see how many shortcuts they can use in two minutes. This game will help reinforce the shortcuts.

Connections

You can apply this lesson to different content areas in the following suggested ways.

- **English language arts:** Have groups of students create a presentation about valuable shortcuts and present to other classrooms.

- **Social science:** Have groups of students study what type of technology was available during one of the

TEACHING TIPS

▸ Remember student voice and choice. Let groups of students become technology explorers and troubleshooters.

▸ Let your students become the tech experts for another class that tries a new project.

space missions, and have the groups compare that to the technology available today.

- **Art:** Have students create posters to hang up in the hallways, highlighting their favorite shortcuts.

Wow: Troubleshooting Device Problems

Familiarity with devices allows students to focus on learning and not get caught up in the mechanics of the devices. The goal of this lesson is to have students become comfortable enough with their device that they know how to troubleshoot problems without it stopping their productivity. This type of problem solving will help students as they encounter ever-growing and ever-changing types of devices outside school.

Process: Rebooting a Device

Use a variety of devices—including a PC, Mac, Chromebook, and iPad—to complete the following four steps for this lesson.

1. Explain to students that when they need to resolve technology problems with a device, they should first reboot it, meaning shutting down a device and restarting it.

2. Show students how to reboot a PC, Mac, and Chromebook using on-screen methods. On an iPad, show them how to press the Start button, slide the screen according to the prompt, and then press the Start button to turn the device back on.

3. In the event that a device becomes non-responsive, students should perform a hard reset. On a PC or Mac, students should press and hold on the power button for about ten seconds until it powers down. After another ten seconds, the device may be powered back on. On an iPad, students should press and hold on the power button and home button at the same time for ten seconds. After another ten seconds, the device may be powered back on. This may resolve the issue.

4. Post a list of rebooting procedures in the classroom.

Learning goal:
I can troubleshoot my device when needed (close out applications, restart it, hard reset it, and ask for assistance after trying to fix it on my own).

TEACHING TIPS

▸ Students should have opportunities to explore their devices. This exploration time will allow students to become more familiar with the features and limitations of their devices.

▸ Teachers should create an anchor chart that outlines the steps to troubleshooting a device. This will allow students to know what steps to take when their device might need troubleshooting.

Connections

You can apply this lesson to different content areas in the following suggested ways.

- **English language arts:** Have groups of students write troubleshooting guides for various devices. These guides should be written for younger K–2 students, and then the groups should present the troubleshooting tips in K–2 classrooms to practice their teaching and listening skills.

- **Mathematics:** Have students research and compare the number of desktop computers, laptops, and tablet devices used in the United States and create an infographic about what they have learned.

- **Science:** Have groups of students research what happens when a device shuts down. Groups can compare and contrast what they learned about different devices by creating a comparison table.

Storing, Sharing, and Managing Online Files

Not only is it important for students to know how devices function, it is also important that they have a good understanding of creating, locating, organizing and managing their files. Students should create a system that is organized and makes sense for themselves. They should be able to create folders that their files are organized in that make navigating to their files fast and easy.

Novice: Creating Online

The goal of this lesson is to help students become comfortable using online tools on any device. Students need to become familiar with this process so they can complete their work in a world increasingly focused around mobile technology, where people are constantly on the go. These skills will prove important as students create more sophisticated products and collaborate globally with groups of students. Students will use these skills in all curricular areas today, tomorrow, and in the future work world.

Learning goal:
I can create an online document or file.

Process: Creating a New Document in Google Drive

To complete the following three lesson steps, we recommend you use Google Docs (https://docs.google.com). If you prefer, you can adapt this process for use with a variety of other options. Options include but are not limited to Google Drawings (https://drawings.google.com), Google Slides (www.google.com/slides/about), and Google Sheets (www.google.com/intl/en_us/sheets/about).

1. Have students open a new file in Google Docs and click on the top-left corner to rename the file from "Untitled Document" to an identifying title.

2. Remind students that documents created in Google Drive automatically save every few minutes, so they do not need to save often themselves. When students finish working on a project, they should just close the browser.

3. Have students share the Google Doc with group members and the teacher using the Share button.

Connections

You can apply this lesson to different content areas in the following suggested ways.

- **English language arts:** Given a research project on a famous person's life, students can collaborate on a Google Doc to research and prepare for a group presentation.

- **Mathematics:** Students can use Google Drawings to demonstrate their understanding of different types of angles by drawing and labeling acute, right, obtuse, and straight angles. Students will share what they have created with the teacher through the class LMS.

- **Social science:** Students can open Google Slides and create several slides in the format of a travel journal, highlighting a region, state, province, or country. Each slide contains a picture and a brief narrative about what the picture includes.

TEACHING TIPS

- If students add pictures to a project, remind them to give credit to the source. See chapter 5 (page 93) for detailed lessons on citing sources.

- Students should be aware that when they share a document with another group member, they are working on *one* document together—not two separate documents—to ensure they work together to accomplish goals and don't accidently delete someone's work.

TECH TIPS

- Use templates that are provided in the software when creating a presentation in Google Slides, Apple Keynote, or Microsoft PowerPoint.

- Make sure students type identifying information as the filename when they save the document—for example, "JohnDoe SSlandformsfeb2018."

- **Science:** While students do an experiment in their lab groups, have them use a shared Google Sheet to record results and identify trends.

- **Art:** Students can create a Google Drawing and use the shape tools to create a modern art masterpiece.

Operational: Locating and Sharing Files

Learning goal:
I can locate files I created and share them when directed by the teacher.

This lesson focuses on helping students organize their files and products for easy access. The goal is that students will create a system that allows them to find their document, share it, review it, and make it better without having to start over every time they stop. They will become efficient workers and get encouraged to check over their work to create the best product possible, because they can easily access their work and make changes.

Process: Sharing Files Using Dropbox

To complete the following two lesson steps, we recommend you use Dropbox (www.dropbox.com), a cloud-based storage system for sharing files. If you prefer, you can adapt this process for use with a variety of other options. Options include but are not limited to Google Drive (www.google.com/drive) and Box (www.box.com/home).

1. The teacher will create a new, free shared classroom Dropbox account.

2. Ask students to locate the file to share on their device and then upload the file to the classroom account the teacher has created. All students will have access to this account once they log in. Using the class account, you can readily view the file.

Connections

You can apply this lesson to different content areas in the following suggested ways.

- **English language arts:** Students can interview a classmate and then type what they learned in a Google Doc. Students locate and share the completed Google Doc with the classmate whom they interviewed. The classmate proofreads the

TEACHING TIPS

- Students need to understand the difference between saving a document to a device (like a laptop, where the document stays on the hard drive of that machine) and saving a document in Google Drive, which they can access from any Internet-enabled device anytime they can connect to the Internet. Lead a class discussion about the concept of saving to a device as compared to saving to Google Drive.

- Let groups of students create a visual map of their understanding of the saving process.

Google Doc to make sure it includes correct information and to check for grammatical errors. They share the document with you through the class LMS.

- **Mathematics:** Students can use a drawing tool such as Notability (www.gingerlabs.com) or the built-in Notes app on Apple devices to demonstrate how to solve a two-digit by two-digit multiplication problem. Students create a text box in which to write out the process they use to solve the problem. Students locate the completed file and share it with another student in the class who proofreads it to see if the process described works.

- **Social science:** A student can create a Google Slides presentation about a historical event and share it with a partner. Both students work on the presentation, collaborating on the content they add. They also share the slide presentation with you through the class LMS.

- **Science:** Students can create an infographic about an element from the periodic table. They share the infographic with a classmate to peer-edit it or assist them with the project's completion.

- **Art:** Students can create a flier using the website Canva (www.canva.com) to highlight a famous artist or painting. They share the flier with a classmate to peer-edit it or assist them with the project's completion.

Wow: Managing and Organizing Files

Having students think about their learning is an important part of metacognition and developing students into 21st century learners. The goal of this lesson is for students to create a portfolio with products that they have chosen to prove their understanding of content. It focuses on students reflecting on and classifying their work. This process will allow students to critically think and learn about how to create a digital portfolio showcasing their work. Students will create a new portfolio folder that will consist of pieces of their work that

Learning goal:
I can manage and organize my files to create a digital portfolio of my learning.

they have already created to showcase their learning throughout the school year.

Process: Managing Digital Folders

To complete the following four lesson steps, we recommend you use Google Drive. If you prefer, you can adapt this process for use with Microsoft Office 365 or a shared drive at school.

1. Have students open their Google Drive and click on New in the upper-left-hand corner.

2. Tell students to select New Folder from the drop-down menu.

3. Students should give the folder a title that describes the content and includes the creation date so they can locate it easily in the future. An example of a portfolio title would be JohnDoePortfolio2017.

4. To move a file that they have created, students click on and drag the file to the new folder.

Connections

You can apply this lesson to different content areas in the following suggested ways.

- **English language arts:** During a unit on narrative writing, students can begin writing several different stories saved in a folder titled Rough Drafts. They should save each document with a name that identifies the topic and date started. As the unit progresses, students choose one story that they write to completion. The students create a folder labeled Digital Portfolio. Once they have edited and finalized their story, they create a copy of the paper and move it to this folder. They may retain the draft files for future publication or delete them.

- **Mathematics:** Students can create a mathematics journal that may contain mathematics vocabulary terms and definitions, a brief biography of a mathematician important to the chapter, and sample problems from each section. At the end of each semester, each student chooses the journal entry that he or she thinks is the best, makes a copy, and adds it to his or her digital portfolio.

TEACHING TIPS

- Having students archive their own work provides a great opportunity for them to lead their own parent, teacher, or student conferences.

- Students should pick their best work to showcase in their portfolios. Teachers may choose to limit portfolios to a certain number of pieces per quarter or term.

TECH TIPS

- When students archive their work, they should make a copy of it and save it to a designated folder. If a file is moved from an existing folder, their work might be harder to locate in the future.

- Students can create a different folder for each academic quarter to show that they meet or exceed standards that teachers can use for reporting purposes.

- **Social science:** When students study current events, have them write a brief news article based on what they learn to demonstrate understanding. At the end of each unit, students choose and make a copy of the best article to add to their digital portfolio.

- **Science:** Have students plan and conduct a science experiment on plant growth. Every week, they take a picture of a plant with a ruler next to it to document growth, and they save it to their Google Drive. At the end of the experiment, the students choose three pictures that best represent the experiment and create an electronic poster with experiment information and results. They then add the poster to their portfolio.

Coding

The term *coding* refers to creating computer code, which is the functional basis for video games and computer apps. Inside and outside the education community, the idea that all students should learn computer coding is receiving a great deal of attention. Coding camps, offered at summer day camps and after-school learning centers, are popping up all over the United States for students as young as five years old. Computer coding is a 21st century skill that students need to understand and be able to manage for their future success. These lessons will help students understand the role that coding has in our everyday lives.

Novice: Recognizing Sequential Steps for Coding

You can use this lesson to have students practice creating steps in a precise order to make something happen or achieve a goal. The purpose of this lesson is to help students understand the role that coding plays in allowing computers to complete tasks. It focuses on the process used to reach the goal, especially how to show options that can take the learner in different directions. Computer programmers need these coding skills to understand the dynamics of software creation.

Learning goal:
I can learn the basics of coding behind an app or a website.

Process: Exploring Coding as Sequential Steps

To complete the following four lesson steps, students will create step-by-step directions to have classmates move from one side of the classroom to the other.

1. Begin with a discussion of basic directions (forward, backward, left, right, turn, and step length).

2. Put students into groups of two or three.

3. Have students write specific directions, guiding a student from one side of the room to the other and helping him or her avoid obstacles (desks, tables, and so on). You may place tape marks on the floor to indicate starting and stopping points.

4. Once students have completed the directions, have them exchange directions with another group for a trial. The new team members highlight directions that confuse them or cause problems in their movement.

Connections

You can apply this lesson to different content areas in the following suggested ways.

- **English language arts:** In a poetry lesson, the teacher will provide a template for writing a poem that must be followed with step-by-step directions.

- **Mathematics:** Students will complete a mathematics task that requires them to follow the order of operations. As a class, discuss how the order of operations and following those steps can be similar to following code.

- **Social science:** Access a coding website to have students draw an example of a house or housing type for a civilization.

- **Science:** Have students experiment with how changing a variable affects the outcome on different coding websites.

- **Art:** Students can use a coding website to draw basic shapes.

TECH TIPS

▸ Visit Code.org (https://code.org) for coding games, activities, and tutorials.

▸ Use the activities at https://code.org/curriculum/course3 to enhance student understanding of coding.

Operational: Applying Coding Skills

You can use this lesson to have students apply what they learned about coding to accomplish a task on a website or app. Coding can open many doors to future accomplishments, making it one of the new basic skills for learners at all levels. Gaming, robotics, research, data collection, computer programming, and many other tasks use coding. An educated student in the 21st century needs to know how to use coding to make tasks simpler and to complete jobs faster.

Process: Learning Scratch Coding

Google CS First (www.cs-first.com/en/home) is a completely free coding site where teachers sign up for a course and receive all the necessary materials to run a club or class that guides students through tutorials to learn Scratch (https://scratch.mit.edu) coding. Scratch coding is a coding language that is easy to use and understand at the beginner level. Use Google CS First to complete the following two steps for this lesson.

1. When your students are ready to explore coding, make sure to plan ahead for this lesson because Google will send supplies, including student passports, progress stickers, and instructions. With the provided supplies, you can track student progress and motivate them to complete more tasks on coding.

2. Have students follow all on-screen directions to complete the course. Remind students that during the course, they need to have two browser tabs open at all times: Google CS First and Scratch. Students log in to both sites with the same account created through the Google CS First site.

Connections

You can apply this lesson to different content areas in the following suggested ways.

- **English language arts:** Prior to a lesson on writing step-by-step procedures, use a simple coding website to show students that if they miss one step, they cannot complete the entire action. This lesson will help students understand that the vocabulary they

Learning goal:
I can apply what I know about coding to accomplish a given task on a website.

TEACHING TIPS

▸ Lead a class discussion about all the occupations that require an understanding of coding.

▸ Students come to class with so many levels of knowledge about coding. Create a help team to assist classmates when they have questions.

▸ To scaffold for students who are unfamiliar with coding, have them explore the games for their grade level at www.tynker.com and move from lower to higher difficulty levels within the games.

TECH TIPS

▸ Students can use a website like Pixel Press (www.projectpixelpress .com) to work offline using paper and pencil to start to understand coding. Next, students can play the online games on the website to practice coding.

▸ Visit Code.org (https:// code.org) for offline activities that help students understand the importance of coding in the 21st century.

Learning goal:

I can choose a coding tool, work through the tutorials, and use the information learned to create a final product.

use and the sequence of the steps are important for someone to understand what they have written.

- **Mathematics:** Use coding sites to have students create geometric shapes.

- **Social science:** Computer coding used to be done with punch cards. Have groups of students research the birth of computer coding and create a presentation including key points in history.

- **Science:** See the Exploratorium activity at www .exploratorium.edu/snacks/breakfast-proteins, and have students work in groups to create a DNA code following this activity.

- **Art:** Use a coding activity like those on the Make Art site (https://art.kano.me/challenges) to draw pictures.

Wow: Creating With Coding

The goal of this lesson is to empower students to write code to create a product. They will use their own voice and choice as they select technology tools. Students will plan, design, build, organize, problem solve, and use many other 21st century skills to succeed in this project. Creating their own product epitomizes self-reliance and innovative thinking, preparing students for college and careers.

Process: Using Coding Apps and Websites

Khan Academy (www.khanacademy.org) is a website filled with educational videos and coding resources. The free site includes lessons, quizzes, and coding and computer-programming activities. Use Khan Academy to complete the following four steps for this lesson. As a teacher, it is also important to understand that some students might want to explore other websites or apps to code with. If you prefer, you can adapt this process for use with a variety of other options. Options include but are not limited to Swift Playgrounds (www.apple.com/swift/playgrounds), Code.org (https://code .org), and Tynker (www.tynker.com). Students should be able to choose the app or website they are most comfortable with in order to complete the task.

1. Have students set up a free Khan Academy account using their Google login.

2. Students will be able to choose a lesson on the site to complete based on their interests. Let students work independently through the courses.

3. Students can add you as their coach, and then you can track students' progress through the different lessons. On the website, the teacher will log in and create a class, generating a class code. Students can enter the class code and are then added to the roster.

4. The teacher now can monitor students' progress as they work on Khan Academy videos and take the assessments that determine readiness to move to the next topic. Each student has a data dashboard for individual reflection as well as a class overview.

Connections

You can apply this lesson to different content areas in the following suggested ways.

- **English language arts:** As a vocabulary activity, students can write specific terms that programs or apps ask for in their coding. Students will do a word study on these terms to define them. This will allow students to internalize these terms and become more fluent in the coding language.

- **Mathematics:** Students can program a robot or droid to move through a maze using coding. Students will need to use coding language and understand mathematics concepts such as degrees, directions, and angles to navigate the robot through the maze.

- **Social science:** Students can research coding and learn how it has assisted communities in staying safe (such as by protecting websites). Students bring the information back to the class and brainstorm ways that what they've learned about coding will help them in the future.

TEACHING TIPS

▸ Students have success using coding websites and apps through trial and error.

▸ As your students at any grade level begin learning how to code, have them work together as partners so they can catch coding errors and problem solve together in order to get their code to work.

TECH TIPS

▸ New coding websites and apps appear all the time. Check an app store for the most up-to-date apps available. Ratings and reviews help you determine the quality of the apps.

▸ If you have a classroom robot, such as Sphero (www.sphero.com/sphero) or Dash (www.make wonder.com/dash), students can change or modify the code using an accompanying app, causing the robot to respond to the code the student created for the robot.

DISCUSSION QUESTIONS

Consider the following questions for personal reflection or in collaborative work with colleagues.

▸ How would you explain Google Drive to someone who has never heard of it?

▸ What is the difference between saving to a digital device and saving to the cloud?

▸ What serves as the best way to have students label their work?

▸ Why should students create a digital portfolio?

▸ What file-management challenges do you face?

▸ What troubleshooting strategies did you learn in this chapter?

▸ How can shortcuts save time, and which ones suggested in this chapter do you like?

▸ What did you learn about coding from this chapter?

▸ Which of the coding projects in this chapter do you think your students will enjoy?

▸ What is one thing from this chapter you will share with your colleagues?

- **Science:** Students can program a robot or droid to complete a task, like moving a pencil, to simulate real-life applications.

- **Art:** Students can research how they may apply coding to art. If applicable, students could try the art form researched.

Conclusion

From getting organized online to learning how to code, we have filled this chapter with practical ways to focus on teaching and learning while using technology. Teachers no longer teach technology in isolation in a computer lab down the hall. We need to make the skills in this chapter part of our core classrooms as students use the technology. Many of the foundational skills in this chapter will save students time as they use technology independently.

Much of the information in this chapter can be helpful for students to share with families. If your students take their devices home, parents might find it helpful to reference the tips in this chapter. The students will become the experts on their devices the more they use them. When students are the experts, they can share that expertise with those around them.

Epilogue

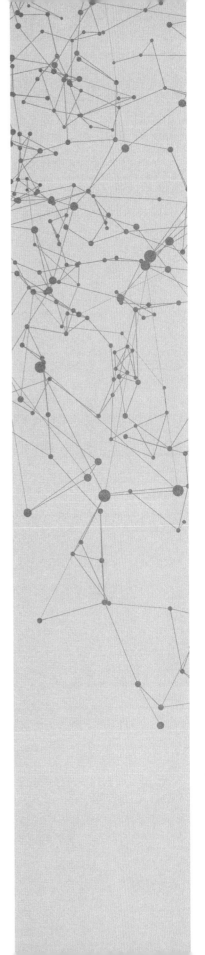

We enjoyed our time researching for and writing this book as we talked about the classrooms of the future. We tested these ideas in our classrooms and came back to report our failures and successes. We modified the lessons, tried them again, and then created our final lessons. We visited each other's classrooms and reflected on what we observed. Each observer reported that he or she first noticed the energy in the room as we worked through a lesson. In all the classrooms, students were scattered in small groups, and some worked independently. Initially, we found it difficult to spot the teachers because they were huddled with small groups.

At first, the rooms looked chaotic, but we hardly found that the case in any of these learning spaces. Every student stayed focused on his or her specific learning goal, and every student we asked could tell us the purpose or objective of the lesson. In the small groups, every member could explain the project and what he or she created. Groups proudly shared how they planned on connecting beyond the walls of the classroom.

The rooms had energy and real joy in the air. In some classrooms, students and teachers worked together in whatever language they could use comfortably with their partners or small groups. No one waited for direct instruction, and when the students completed the tasks, they each knew how to transition to the next project without waiting for an adult. If students needed redirection, they turned to a classmate instead of interrupting the teacher who was working with a small group.

As we reflected, we realized we had heard the word *fun* a lot in these rooms. One classroom had a green screen and lights, and groups of students created book trailers with these resources. Students could tell us about the technology choices they made to complete their book trailers and why they selected certain apps or software programs. These students all functioned as architects of their own learning. We found it so refreshing to watch.

Students made their voice and choice evident everywhere. Students made informed decisions about their learning paths, instead of selecting from menus with only a few options. They liked to talk about how their work reached an authentic audience and why they liked that. In one of the classrooms, a group of students explained that they liked to see how many times their work got reposted on social media.

We write about NOW classrooms to help readers visualize what can happen when we involve students in their learning journey with or without technology. Creating NOW classrooms can be done; we have seen it happen, and the movement is growing every time a teacher supports student voice and choice and teachers and students become partners in the process of learning together.

Re-Energizing Teaching and Learning With the Four Cs

It is exciting to see such robust teaching and learning in action. These rooms buzzed with energy, and each student stayed engaged. This did not happen because of a device; this happened with teachers' careful planning and willingness to let go of the control to navigate every step of the learning process for the students. We know that real transformational change happens around teaching and learning with the support of digital devices when appropriate. Students were energized because they took charge of what they were doing and they had an authentic audience for their final product. It excited them to share their work beyond the walls of the classroom. This work mattered to them.

When we talk about the four Cs of communication, collaboration, critical thinking, and creativity, we mean we want to see this kind of authentic student creation in classrooms. Every day, every educator should focus on creating lifelong learners who love to tackle problems and challenges—especially hard, real-life problems. Our students crave collaboration, and outside of school, they constantly stay connected. Let's bring that energy into every learning opportunity we plan for. We have no idea what jobs these students will have in the future, but we can help them practice the four Cs when they are with us, so when those jobs emerge, our students will know how to work with others on the very real problems of the future.

Looking Forward

We hope your students have collected critical skills for future success as you have introduced the lessons' various projects. We covered a lot in this book, and all the grade-level books have the same organization so you can easily pick up on the next one and continue to develop your skills.

We wrote this series of books to help all teachers who might have to close their own gap with personal professional development. We hope in reading this book, you have ideas you can immediately use in your classroom. Continue to use the projects and lessons in the book to differentiate your teaching to match your learners' needs. Bring joy to your classroom. Give your students voice and choice, and what quality projects they produce will surprise you.

We know we have work to do, but we have started the process. When we visited each other's classrooms, we walked by far too many classrooms in which the teacher stood at the whiteboard and students sat still. To spread the joy, teachers need quality professional development and clear expectations about change. Administrators also need specific professional development so they can coach teachers about changing instructional practice. Just because students and teachers have devices open in the classroom doesn't mean that quality teaching and learning happen. We need to keep moving forward, and we can do this. Share your joy and new discoveries—don't give up!

Appendix:
Glossary of Tools
and Terms

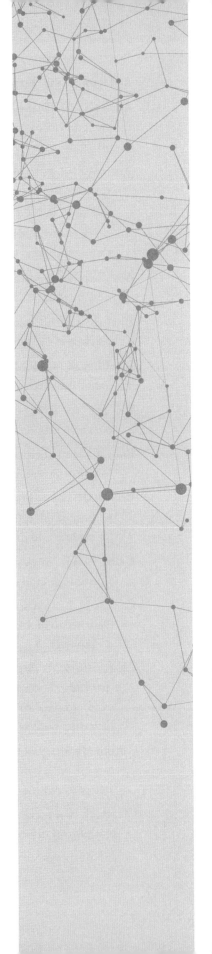

This author team has carefully curated this appendix of all the digital tools and resources mentioned in this book along with other favorites that we could not fit in the text. We provide URLs for these websites and a short description about each tool's purpose or use. Visit **go.SolutionTree.com /technology** to download a free reproducible version of this appendix and access live links to these sites. As you are reading the book, you can use the active hyperlinks to explore the digital resources we provided for you. Feel free to share this reproducible with colleagues who are interested in teaching and learning with technology.

Academic Kids (http://academickids.com): A free online encyclopedia for students

Adobe Spark (https://spark.adobe.com): A free website for designing graphics, images, videos, and webpages, with templates that make it easy for teachers and students to create projects

Animoto (https://animoto.com): A video-creation website and app with limited free features and options for educator accounts (see https://animoto.com/education /classroom)

Audacity (www.audacityteam.org): Free software for a Mac or Windows computer that makes editing complex audio clips possible

AutoRap (www.smule.com/apps): A free iPad- and iPhone-only app, available to download from the App Store that allows users to generate rap songs

Bitly (https://bitly.com): A tool for shortening URLs to make it easier for people to reach specific webpages

Blackboard (www.blackboard.com): A learning management system that is fee based and often used at the higher education level

Blogger (www.blogger.com): Google's free, easy-to-use online blogging platform, packed with features, including the ability to leave comments for a blog's author

Book Creator (https://bookcreator.com): A tool available on the web or as an app for creating ebooks on iPads, Android tablets, and Windows tablets

BrainPOP (www.brainpop.com): An animated educational site for students filled with short educational videos, including free content and paid subscription access for schools and districts

Canva (www.canva.com): A website with free and premium features to create stunning graphics and visual content

Canvas K–12 (www.canvaslms.com/k-12): An LMS software tool for organizing students' digital work and managing, tracking, and reporting educational data and courses

ChatterPix Kids (www.duckduckmoose.com/educational-iphone-itouch-apps -for-kids/chatterpixkids): An iPad- and iPhone-only app that students can use to record their voice, select a picture to attach the recording to, and play the recording back as if the object says what the students recorded

Chrome (www.google.com/chrome): A web browser developed by Google that you can use on any device and that has additional features such as extensions and the ability to sync bookmarks across all devices

Classkick (www.classkick.com): An app that allows teachers to see what students are working on in real time on individual, internet-connected devices

CodeCombat (https://codecombat.com): A web-gaming tool for learning programming

Code.org (https://code.org): A website for learning coding and programming on iPads, Chromebooks, and Android devices

Common Sense (www.commonsense.org): A collection of articles, videos, and resources to use for teaching digital citizenship; connects with offshoots Common Sense Media (www.commonsensemedia.org) and Common Sense Education (www.commonsense.org/education)

Crunchzilla (www.crunchzilla.com): A website that offers interactive tutorials to teach coding

D2L (www.d2l.com): A learning management system from Brightspace, short for Desire2Learn

Digital Compass (www.digitalcompass.org): An app created through Common Sense Media for grades 6–8 to help students navigate the Internet safely

Digital Passport (www.digitalpassport.org): An app created through Common Sense Media for grades 3–5 to help students navigate through different resources about digital citizenship and Internet safety

DinoSearch (www.dinosearch.com): A safe search engine for students

Do Ink (www.doink.com): An iPad- and iPhone-only app for creating green-screen videos that has free features as well as premium features

Dotstorming (https://dotstorming.com): A free app groups can use to vote online through their own Dotstorming board

Dropbox (www.dropbox.com): A free service for storing and sharing files

Easel.ly (www.easel.ly): A template-based website with free and premium features for easily creating stunning infographics

EasyBib (www.easybib.com): A website and app for easily creating citations, with free options as well as premium features

Edge (www.microsoft.com/en-us/windows/microsoft-edge): A web browser developed by Microsoft that has replaced Internet Explorer

Edmodo (www.edmodo.com): One of the many learning management systems available

Educreations (www.educreations.com): An interactive screencast whiteboard with free and premium options that students can use to record their learning

Encyclopaedia Britannica (www.britannica.com): A free online encyclopedia

Encyclopedia.com (www.encyclopedia.com): A tool for gathering research and information

Excel (https://products.office.com/en-us/excel): A spreadsheet program that you can use on both Apple and Windows devices and that makes up part of the Microsoft Office suite as well as the online Microsoft Office 365 subscription service

Explain Everything (https://explaineverything.com): A paid collaborative and interactive whiteboard website and app for Android and Apple devices as well as a Google Chrome extension

Exploratorium (www.exploratorium.edu): A website with educational tools that the Exploratorium science museum in San Francisco, California, maintains

Facebook (www.facebook.com): A social media network to connect with others using text and pictures, either for professional or personal use, for those age 13 or older

Flickr (www.flickr.com): A free website for searching for images that includes Explore functions and a Creative Commons category with images in the public domain

Fluency Tutor (https://fluency.texthelp.com/Chrome/Get): An extension in Google Chrome that you need to add to student devices to record students as they read on a computer or tablet

Fodey (www.fodey.com): A website with various templates that generate products for download, such as newspaper stories, movie clapper boards, cartoons, and more

Formative (https://goformative.com): A free website for collecting information in the form of a drawing, text, or multiple-choice response for a quick formative assessment that gives immediate individual feedback to students

GarageBand (www.apple.com/mac/garageband): Apple-only software and an iPad and iPhone app for making music, recording narrations, and creating new audio projects

Genius Hour: Time set aside for students to research and learn about whatever interests them

Genius Hour Blog Posts (www.geniushour.com/genius-hour-blog-posts): A blog with ideas about getting started with and holding Genius Hour in a classroom

Genius Hour Ideas (www.geniushour.com/2013/03/31/genius-hour-ideas): A webpage listing topics to use for research during Genius Hour

Glogster (http://edu.glogster.com): A subscription website where students can make *Glogs*, or multimedia mashups, to create a final product

Google (www.google.com): A search engine developed by Google

Google Classroom (https://classroom.google.com): A file management system with some features of an LMS that allows classrooms to share announcements and documents and conduct discussions

Google CS First (www.cs-first.com/en/home): A free coding site where teachers sign up for a course and receive all the necessary materials to run a club or class that guides students through tutorials to learn Scratch coding

Google Docs (https://docs.google.com): A word processing tool in Google Drive, a part of the G Suite for Education, for creating and editing documents independently or in collaborative groups; available to all teachers and students who are members of the Google domain through their school, often called a *Google School*

Google Drawings (https://drawings.google.com): A drawing app within G Suite for Education

Google Drive (www.google.com/drive): A cloud-based storage platform that can store and sync files across multiple devices using a single login

Google for Education (www.google.com/intl/en_us/edu): An overarching term for all the Google products that a school system has available for staff and student use

Google Forms (www.google.com/intl/en_us/forms/about): A survey and form-making app within G Suite for Education

Google Hangouts (https://hangouts.google.com): A unified communications service that allows members to initiate and participate in text, voice, and video chats either one-on-one or in a group and that is built into Google+ and Gmail and available as an app for Apple and Android devices

Google Maps (https://maps.google.com): Part of Google that students can use to generate maps to support their learning

Google My Maps (www.google.com/maps/d): A Google service where students create their own maps and insert place markers with additional data about a topic

Google Photos (https://photos.google.com): A photo storage, organization, and editing website, formerly called Picasa

Google Sheets (www.google.com/intl/en_us/sheets/about): A spreadsheet app within G Suite for Education that supports common spreadsheet functions such as data entry, sorting, number calculation, and chart creation

Google Sites (https://sites.google.com): A free website builder created by Google

Google Slides (www.google.com/slides/about): A web-based presentation creator available in G Suite for Education that allows users to insert images, text, charts, and videos, as well as modify transitions, layouts, and backgrounds

Google URL Shortener (https://goo.gl): A tool for shortening URLs on the web to make it easier for someone to reach a specific webpage as quickly as possible

Google+ Communities (http://plus.google.com/communities): A social networking community where educators can connect by posting ideas, questions, and requests to connect with other classrooms through Skype, Google Hangouts, and blogs

Haiku Deck (www.haikudeck.com): An online presentation tool for creating slides with beautiful images and limited text that includes a few free features and a premium version

hyperdoc: A digital document that contains links to various online resources to save time as students quickly navigate to predetermined links and that teachers can share with students on the class LMS as active, clickable links

iMovie (www.apple.com/imovie): An Apple video creation app only available on an iPhone, an iPad, or a Mac computer

Infobase Learning (http://online.infobase.com/HRC/Browse/Product/8): An online database with videos and primary documents for student use

Infogram (https://infogram): A website with free and premium features for creating infographics using the data students collect

Infotopia (www.infotopia.info): A safe search engine for students

i-nigma (www.i-nigma.com/i-nigmahp.html): A QR code scanner website

Instagram (www.instagram.com): A social media network for people to connect with others predominantly through pictures with short captions

interactive whiteboard: An interactive display board, often referred to as a *SMART Board* even though many different manufacturers exist, including SMART Technologies, Promethean, and Mimio

Jumpshare (https://jumpshare.com): A free service for storing and sharing photos, documents, and videos

Kahoot! (https://getkahoot.com): A free website for creating quizzes and answering the questions from any digital device

Kevin Honeycutt (http://kevinhoneycutt.org): A site with online collaborative projects created by educator Kevin Honeycutt, with many PBL opportunities for students and tool ideas to spark student and teacher creativity

Keynote (www.apple.com/keynote): An Apple presentation tool

Khan Academy (www.khanacademy.org): A screencast tutorial website for students to watch videos and check their understanding of concepts

Kidblog (https://kidblog.org/home): A website where students can publish and share their learning in a secure environment

Kiddle (www.kiddle.co): A visual search engine for students

KidRex (www.kidrex.org): An age-appropriate search engine for students

Kidtopia (www.kidtopia.info): A safe, custom Google search engine for elementary students

KidzSearch (www.kidzsearch.com): An age-appropriate search engine for students

Kinder Art (www.kinderart.com/arthistory): An age-appropriate site students can use to research the history of art

Kizoa (www.kizoa.com/School): A website for creating multimedia movies with images and music

learning management system (LMS): Software used to manage, track, and report educational data and courses

Library of Congress (www.loc.gov): The main research arm of the U.S. Congress, filled with collections of resources grouping primary source documents of all types

LINER (http://getliner.com): An extension available for most web browsers that allows users to read, highlight, and share across different websites to help students organize research

Lucidpress (www.lucidpress.com): A website where students and teachers can create stunning brochures, flyers, digital magazines, newsletters, and reports, with nothing to install on any device and the capability to add all types of media to a project with a simple drag-and-drop interface

Magisto (www.magisto.com): A website and an app available for Apple and Android that turns video and images into movies

Make Art (https://art.kano.me/challenges): A coding website with tutorials to teach the user how to code and create artwork

Math Playground (www.mathplayground.com/mathprogramming.html): A website filled with mathematics resources and coding activities and games

Microsoft Office (https://products.office.com/en-US): A suite of software that contains Word, PowerPoint, Excel, and other Microsoft programs

Microsoft Publisher (https://office.microsoft.com/publisher): Part of the Microsoft Office suite as well as the online Microsoft Office 365 service, which you can use on both Apple and Windows devices, containing templates to create items such as newsletters, posters, and other digital content

Mimio (www.mimio.com/en-AP.aspx): One brand of interactive whiteboards and software solutions

Moodle (https://moodle.org): A free, open-source learning management system

Mozilla Firefox (www.mozilla.org/en-US/firefox/new): A web browser the global nonprofit company Mozilla created

myON (www.myon.com): A reading platform based on student interest, reading level, and ratings of books

Mystery Skype (https://education.microsoft.com/skype-in-the-classroom /mystery-skype): A service offered on the Skype website to help teachers connect and collaborate with another unknown classroom

NetSmartz (www.netsmartz.org): A website with resources teachers can use to support digital citizenship education in the classroom

Newsela (https://newsela.com): A site with leveled news, primary sources, standards-aligned formative assessments, and more that includes free content and premium features

The NOW Classrooms Project (http://nowclassrooms.com/about): A website about the entire NOW Classrooms Project, including the *NOW Classrooms* blog and details about the book series

Otus (https://otus.com): A classroom LMS that integrates data from third parties to get a more comprehensive snapshot about student growth

Padlet (https://padlet.com): A digital bulletin board for student collaborative projects that students join through a code the teacher provides

Paint (http://microsoft_paint.en.downloadastro.com): A Microsoft tool for creating digital drawings that PC operating systems include

Pearson SuccessNet (www.pearsonsuccessnet.com): The online portal for many of Pearson's digital content solutions

Photoshop (www.adobe.com/photoshop): An image-editing program that can be accessed through the Adobe Creative Cloud for a monthly fee

PicCollage (https://pic-collage.com): A free media mashup app (with in-app purchases) for all devices that allows students to add pictures, stickers, and backgrounds and use various templates

PicMonkey (www.picmonkey.com): A free online image editor

Piktochart (https://piktochart.com): A template-driven website with free and premium features for easily creating stunning infographics

Pixel Press (www.projectpixelpress.com): A tool used to learn coding and programming

Pixlr (https://pixlr.com/editor): A website used to edit images for free

PlayPosit (www.playposit.com): A free interactive website that allows teachers to post instructional videos while embedding questions throughout to receive feedback and give immediate feedback to their students on a lesson

Plickers (https://plickers.com): A website and a free app for Apple and Android devices teachers can use to conduct quick formative assessments by scanning students' multiple-choice response codes in real time

PowerPoint (https://products.office.com/en-us/powerpoint): Part of the Microsoft Office suite as well as the online Microsoft Office 365 subscription, which you can use on both Apple and Windows devices to create presentations

PowerSchool Learning (formerly Haiku Learning) (www.powerschool.com/solutions/lms): A learning management system with limited free access as well as premium features

Prezi (https://prezi.com): An online presentation creation tool

Projects by Jen (https://projectsbyjen.com): A site with different online collaborative projects created by educator Jen Wagner that teachers can join

Promethean (www.prometheanworld.com): One brand of interactive whiteboards and software solutions

Publisher (https://products.office.com/en-us/publisher): Part of the Microsoft Office suite as well as the online Microsoft Office 365 subscription, which you can use on both Apple and Windows devices, with templates to create things like newsletters, posters, and other digital content

QR Reader (https://itunes.apple.com/us/app/qr-reader-for-iphone/id368494609?mt=8): A free QR code reader for the iPhone

Quizizz (https://quizizz.com): A free website for creating and storing quizzes that has leaderboards, music, and more to engage learners

ReadWriteThink (www.readwritethink.org): A website that has many helpful tools for writing

Safari (www.apple.com/safari): A web browser Apple developed that can only be used on Mac operating systems

Safe Kids (www.safekids.com): A free website filled with digital citizenship resources

Safe Search Kids (www.safesearchkids.com): A search engine for students

sandbox: A term for a virtual space in which learners can securely play with and explore new or untested software without judgment

Scan (www.scan.me): A QR code generator and reader

Scholastic News (http://magazines.scholastic.com): An online, age-appropriate news site for students, organized and published by Scholastic, offering free stories as well as a paid classroom subscription

Schoology (www.schoology.com): A learning management system containing a discussion board where students can write posts in response to an ongoing discussion

Scratch (https://scratch.mit.edu): A free coding language and online community developed by MIT that acts as the basis for Google CS First courses and tutorials

ScratchJr (www.scratchjr.org): A tool for learning a programming language

screencast: A recording of a digital screen with audio added to explain a concept

Screencastify (www.screencastify.com): An extension of the Chrome browser, or an application that users can install and run through the Chrome browser, used to create screencast movies

Screencast-O-Matic (https://screencast-o-matic.com): A free website with an inexpensive pro upgrade that teachers and students can use to create screencasts

screenshot: An image of the display on a computer screen

Seesaw (http://web.seesaw.me): A site and app for creating student-driven digital portfolios, with free basic features, premium advanced features, and school versions

sketchnoting: A term for taking notes as a visual story with words and pictures to connect and communicate new ideas (visit Sketchnote Army [http://sketchnotearmy.com] to see examples)

SketchUp (www.sketchup.com): A tool used to model in 3-D that includes free and premium features

Skitch (https://evernote.com/products/skitch): An app for taking and annotating pictures

Skype (www.skype.com/en): A video and instant messaging app that you can install on any type of device to collaborate with other classes and all types of experts

SMART Technologies (https://home.smarttech.com): One brand of interactive whiteboards and software solutions

Smithsonian Institution (www.si.edu): The website for all of the Smithsonian museums

Smithsonian Learning Lab (https://learninglab.si.edu): A database of information for students to use as they research topics

Smithsonian Magazine (www.smithsonianmag.com): The magazine about the Smithsonian museums

Snapchat (www.snapchat.com): An image-messaging and multimedia social networking app, for users age 13 and older, where students can create stories and share them with their followers

Socrative (www.socrative.com): A tool to survey and assess progress that includes free and premium features

Stop Motion Studio (www.cateater.com/stopmotionstudio): A free app for creating stop-motion videos

Stormboard (https://stormboard.com): A collaborative online brainstorming environment students can access from any device

SurveyMonkey (www.surveymonkey.com): A website with free and premium features for creating and circulating surveys

Swift Playgrounds (https://developer.apple.com/swift/playgrounds): An iPad-only app for learning Swift code in a fun, interactive way to help students understand app creation

Symbaloo (www.symbaloo.com): A social bookmarking website to organize research tools for students to access that works similarly to a hyperdoc but has much more visual appeal

Teaching Channel (www.teachingchannel.org): An online community where teachers can watch videos and connect with other teachers about strategies to help students

Tellagami (https://tellagami.com): An Apple-only app where students create an avatar, record a sound clip, and have a character play back the recording with added gestures

ThemeSpark (www.themespark.net): A website for creating rubrics for projects

Thinglink (www.thinglink.com): A website with free and premium features for annotating images to demonstrate learning

TinyURL (https://tinyurl.com): A URL shortener that makes smaller, more manageable website addresses for student use

TodaysMeet (https://todaysmeet.com): A tool that provides a backchannel for participants to comment and provide input without disrupting a presentation

TouchCast (www.touchcast.com): A smart video production website and app for both Apple and Android devices that allows students to create and share interactive videos

TweenTribune (www.tweentribune.com): A Smithsonian site featuring free leveled news articles, primary sources, and quizzes

Twitter (https://twitter.com): A popular social media site for communicating short messages through text and multimedia (We encourage the use of a teacher or classroom account.)

Tynker (www.tynker.com): A tool used to learn coding, which includes free and premium features

Video Star (http://videostarapp.com): A free app for iPads and iPhones designed to make music videos, with hundreds of built-in effects and filters

VoiceThread (https://voicethread.com): A paid subscription website where teachers can set up an online collaborative space for students to create video, voice, and text commenting

WatchKnowLearn (www.watchknowlearn.org): A website that contains free educational videos

Weebly (www.weebly.com): A template-based website builder with free and premium features

WeVideo (www.wevideo.com): A video creation and video-sharing tool that uses cloud-based video-editing software and includes free and premium features

Wikipedia (https://en.wikipedia.org): A free online encyclopedia that is open to users to add information (causing some to question its credibility as a primary research source) that is useful for finding additional sources of information

Wikispaces (www.wikispaces.com): An online collaboration platform that users can open or close to a global audience

Word (https://products.office.com/en-us/word): Part of the Microsoft Office suite as well as part of the online Microsoft Office 365 subscription that you can use on both Apple and Windows devices for word processing

Word Art (https://wordart.com): A tag cloud generator formerly called Tagul

Wordle (www.wordle.net): A tag cloud generator

WordPress (https://wordpress.com): A free blogging website

Yahoo! (www.yahoo.com): A search engine developed by Yahoo!

YouTube (www.youtube.com): A video platform for publishing and viewing video content

References and Resources

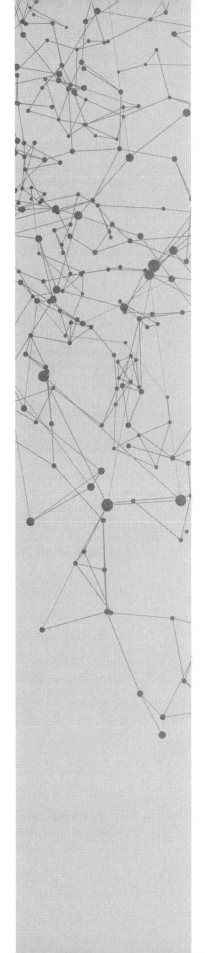

Alber, R. (2012, December 31). *Deeper learning: A collaborative classroom is key* [Blog post]. Accessed at www.edutopia.org /blog/deeper-learning-collaboration-key-rebecca-alber on January 16, 2017.

Anderson, L. W., & Krathwohl, D. R. (Eds.). (2001). *A taxonomy for learning, teaching, and assessing: A revision of Bloom's taxonomy of educational objectives* (Complete ed.). New York: Longman.

Azzam, A. M. (2014). Motivated to learn: A conversation with Daniel Pink. *Educational Leadership, 72*(1), 12–17.

Bebell, D., & Kay, R. (2010). One to one computing: A summary of the quantitative results from the Berkshire Wireless Learning Initiative. *Journal of Technology, Learning, and Assessment, 9*(2). Accessed at http://ejournals .bc.edu/ojs/index.php/jtla/article/view/1607/1462 on April 3, 2017.

Bebell, D., & O'Dwyer, L. (2010). Educational outcomes and research from 1:1 computing settings. *Journal of Technology, Learning, and Assessment, 9*(1). Accessed at http://ejournals.bc.edu/ojs/index.php/jtla/article/view/1606 on April 3, 2017.

Belgrad, S., Burke, K., & Fogarty, R. (2008). *The portfolio connection: Student work linked to standards* (3rd ed.). Thousand Oaks, CA: Corwin Press.

Bender, W. N. (2012). *Differentiating instruction for students with learning disabilities: New best practices for general and special educators* (3rd ed.). Thousand Oaks, CA: Corwin Press.

Block, J. (2014, October 30). *Student choice leads to student voice* [Blog post]. Accessed at www.edutopia.org/blog/student-choice-leads-to-voice-joshua-block on January 16, 2017.

Bransford, J. D., Brown, A. L., & Cocking, R. R. (Eds.). (1999). *How people learn: Brain, mind, experience, and school.* Washington, DC: National Academy Press.

Briggs, S. (n.d.). *50 ways to empower students in a connected world.* Accessed at www.teachthought.com/the-future-of-learning/50-ways-empower-students-connected-world on February 13, 2017.

Brock, A., & Hundley, H. (2016). *The growth mindset coach: A teacher's month-by-month handbook for empowering students to achieve.* Berkeley, CA: Ulysses Press.

Brookhart, S. M. (2008). *How to give effective feedback to your students.* Alexandria, VA: Association for Supervision and Curriculum Development.

Brookhart, S. M. (2012). Preventing feedback fizzle. *Educational Leadership*, *70*(1), 24–29.

Burgess, D. (2012). *Teach like a pirate: Increase student engagement, boost your creativity, and transform your life as an educator.* San Diego, CA: Burgess Consulting.

Chappuis, J. (2012). "How am I doing?" *Educational Leadership*, *70*(1), 36–41.

Children's Online Privacy Protection Act of 1998, 15 U.S.C. §§ 6501–6505 (2012).

Concordia University–Portland. (2013, April 25). *Five ways to teach research skills to elementary school children* [Blog post]. Accessed at http://education.cu-portland.edu/blog/reference-material/five-ways-to-teach-research-skills-to-elementary-school-children on January 16, 2017.

Costa, A. L. (2008). *The school as a home for the mind: Creating mindful curriculum, instruction, and dialogue* (2nd ed.). Thousand Oaks, CA: Corwin Press.

Couros, G. (2015). *The innovator's mindset: Empower learning, unleash talent, and lead a culture of creativity.* San Diego, CA: Burgess Consulting.

Daily Mail Reporter. (2011, February 3). It must be true, I read it on the Internet: Elusive 'tree octopus' proves how gullible web generation is. *Daily Mail.* Accessed at www.dailymail.co.uk/news/article-1352929/Endangered-tree-octopus-proves-students-believe-read-Internet.html on July 5, 2017.

Danielson, C. (2007). *Enhancing professional practice: A framework for teaching* (2nd ed.). Alexandria, VA: Association for Supervision and Curriculum Development.

Davis, M. (2012). *How collaborative learning leads to student success.* Accessed at www.edutopia.org/stw-collaborative-learning-college-prep on January 16, 2017.

Digital footprint. (n.d.). In *Dictionary.com.* Accessed at www.dictionary.com/browse/digital-footprint?s=t on January 16, 2017.

DuFour, R., DuFour, R., & Eaker, R. (2008). *Revisiting Professional Learning Communities at Work: New insights for improving schools.* Bloomington, IN: Solution Tree Press.

DuFour, R., DuFour, R., Eaker, R., & Karhanek, G. (2010). *Raising the bar and closing the gap: Whatever it takes.* Bloomington, IN: Solution Tree Press.

Duke, N. K. (2016, August 15). *Evaluating websites as information sources* [Blog post]. Accessed at www.edutopia.org/blog/evaluating-websites-as-information-sources-nell-k-duke on January 16, 2017.

Dweck, C. S. (2006). *Mindset: The new psychology of success.* New York: Random House.

Edutopia. (2007). *Why do we need technology integration?* Accessed at www.edutopia.org/technology-integration-guide-importance on January 16, 2017.

Ferriter, W. M. (2014, November 11). *Are there WRONG ways to use technology?* [Blog post]. Accessed at www.solutiontree.com/blog/wrong-ways-to-use-technology on February 13, 2017.

Ferriter, W. M., & Garry, A. (2010). *Teaching the iGeneration: 5 easy ways to introduce essential skills with web 2.0 tools.* Bloomington, IN: Solution Tree Press.

Ferriter, W. M., Ramsden, J. T., & Sheninger, E. C. (2011). *Communicating and connecting with social media.* Bloomington, IN: Solution Tree Press.

Fisher, D., & Frey, N. (2012). Making time for feedback. *Educational Leadership, 70*(1), 42–46.

Fullan, M., & Donnelly, K. (2013, July 16). *Alive in the swamp: Assessing digital innovations in education.* Accessed at www.nesta.org.uk/publications/alive-swamp-assessing-digital-innovations-education on February 13, 2017.

Fullan, M., & Langworthy, M. (2013). *Towards a new end: New pedagogies for deep learning.* Seattle, WA: Collaborative Impact.

Gerido, L., & Curran, M. C. (2014). Enhancing science instruction through student-created PowerPoint presentations. *American Biology Teacher, 76*(9), 627–631.

Godin, S. (2008). *Tribes: We need you to lead us.* New York: Portfolio.

Gordon, J. (2007). *The energy bus: 10 rules to fuel your life, work, and team with positive energy.* Hoboken, NJ: Wiley.

Graham, M. J. (2013). *Google Apps meets Common Core.* Thousand Oaks, CA: Corwin Press.

Gregory, G. H. (2008). *Differentiated instructional strategies in practice: Training, implementation, and supervision* (2nd ed.). Thousand Oaks, CA: Corwin Press.

Gregory, G. H., & Chapman, C. M. (2013). *Differentiated instructional strategies: One size doesn't fit all* (3rd ed.). Thousand Oaks, CA: Corwin Press.

Hattie, J. (2009). *Visible learning: A synthesis of over 800 meta-analyses relating to achievement.* London: Routledge.

Hattie, J. (2012a). Know thy impact. *Educational Leadership, 70*(1), 18–23.

Hattie, J. (2012b). *Visible learning for teachers: Maximizing impact on learning.* London: Routledge.

Hernandez, M. (2015, September 16). *Empowering students through multimedia storytelling* [Blog post]. Accessed at www.edutopia.org/blog/empowering-students-through -multimedia-storytelling-michael-hernandez on January 16, 2017.

Hertz, M. B. (2012, December 3). *Digital native vs digital citizen?: Examining a dangerous stereotype* [Blog post]. Accessed at www.edutopia.org/blog/digital-native-digitial -citizen-stereotype-mary-beth-hertz on January 16, 2017.

Hertz, M. B. (2015, October 21). *How to teach Internet safety to younger elementary students* [Blog post]. Accessed at www.edutopia.org/blog/Internet-safety-younger-elementary -mary-beth-hertz on January 16, 2017.

International Society for Technology in Education. (2008). *ISTE standards for teachers.* Accessed at www.iste.org/standards/standards/standards-for-teachers on April 4, 2017.

International Society for Technology in Education. (2016). *ISTE standards for students.* Accessed at www.iste.org/standards/standards/for-students-2016 on April 4, 2017.

Kesler, C. (2013, March 31). *Genius Hour blog: Genius Hour ideas* [Blog post]. Accessed at www.geniushour.com/2013/03/31/genius-hour-ideas on April 10, 2017.

Knutson, C. (2014, June 10). *Preventing summer slide: Why not try Internet research?* [Blog post]. Accessed at www.edutopia.org/blog/preventing-summer-slide-Internet -research-cathy-knutson on January 16, 2017.

Miller, A. (2016, January 25). *Voice and choice: It's more than just "what"* [Blog post]. Accessed at www.edutopia.org/blog/voice-and-choice-more-than-what-andrew-miller on January 16, 2017.

Miller, M. (2015). *Ditch that textbook: Free your teaching and revolutionize your classroom.* San Diego, CA: Burgess Consulting.

Nesloney, T., & Welcome, A. (2016). *Kids deserve it!: Pushing boundaries and challenging conventional thinking.* San Diego, CA: Burgess Consulting.

November, A. (2012). *Who owns the learning?: Preparing students for success in the digital age.* Bloomington, IN: Solution Tree Press.

Partnership for 21st Century Skills. (2011). *Framework for 21st century learning.* Accessed at www.p21.org/storage/documents/1.__p21_framework_2-pager.pdf on April 6, 2017.

Pearlman, B. (2009). Making 21st century schools: Creating learner-centered schoolplaces/workplaces for a new culture of students at work. *Educational Technology, 49*(5), 14–19.

Pogrow, S. (2009). *Teaching content outrageously: How to captivate all students and accelerate learning, grades 4–12.* San Francisco: Jossey-Bass.

Robinson, K. (2006, February). *Ken Robinson: Do schools kill creativity?* [Video file]. Accessed at www.ted.com/talks/ken_robinson_says_schools_kill_creativity on February 13, 2017.

Robinson, K. (2009). *The element: How finding your passion changes everything.* New York: Viking.

Robinson, K., & Aronica, L. (2015). *Creative schools: The grassroots revolution that's transforming education.* New York: Viking.

Sanfelippo, J., & Sinanis, T. (2016). *Hacking leadership: 10 ways great leaders inspire learning that teachers, students, and parents love.* South Euclid, OH: Times 10.

Schiller, S. Z. (2009). Practicing learner-centered teaching: Pedagogical design and assessment of a second life project. *Journal of Information Systems Education, 20*(3), 369–381.

Serravallo, J. (2015). *The reading strategies book: Your everything guide to developing skilled readers.* Portsmouth, NH: Heinemann.

Solarz, P. (2015). *Learn like a pirate: Empower your students to collaborate, lead, and succeed.* San Diego, CA: Burgess Consulting.

Speck, M., & Knipe, C. (2001). *Why can't we get it right?: Professional development in our schools.* Thousand Oaks, CA: Corwin Press.

Suvansri, B. (2016, April 8). *Creating meaningful global connections* [Blog post]. Accessed at www.edutopia.org/blog/creating-meaningful-global-connections-bridget-suvansri on January 16, 2017.

Taranto, G., Dalbon, M., & Gaetano, J. (2011). Academic social networking brings web 2.0 technologies to the middle grades. *Middle School Journal, 42*(5), 12–19.

Tate, M. L. (2010). *Worksheets don't grow dendrites: 20 instructional strategies that engage the brain* (2nd ed.). Thousand Oaks, CA: Corwin Press.

Tate, M. L. (2012). *"Sit and get" won't grow dendrites: 20 professional learning strategies that engage the adult brain* (2nd ed.). Thousand Oaks, CA: Corwin Press.

Tovani, C. (2012). Feedback is a two-way street. *Educational Leadership, 70*(1), 48–51.

Tynker. (n.d.). *Four reasons why kids should learn to program* [Blog post]. Accessed at www.tynker.com/blog/articles/ideas-and-tips/four-reasons-why-kids-should-learn-programming on January 16, 2017.

Vincent, T. (2014, August 14). *Plan a better iMovie trailer with these PDFs* [Blog post]. Accessed at http://learninginhand.com/blog/2014/8/6/plan-a-better-imovie-trailer -with-these-pdfs on April 4, 2017.

Visible Learning. (n.d.). *Hattie ranking: 195 influences and effect sizes related to student achievement.* Accessed at http://visible-learning.org/hattie-ranking-influences-effect -sizes-learning-achievement on December 3, 2013.

Wagner, T. (2012). *Creating innovators: The making of young people who will change the world.* New York: Scribner.

Wiliam, D. (2011). *Embedded formative assessment.* Bloomington, IN: Solution Tree Press.

Williams, J. (2015, October 16). *Collaborative learning spaces: Classrooms that connect to the world* [Blog post]. Accessed at www.edutopia.org/blog/collaborative-learning-spaces -connect-to-world-jennifer-williams-fran-siracusa on January 16, 2017.

Index

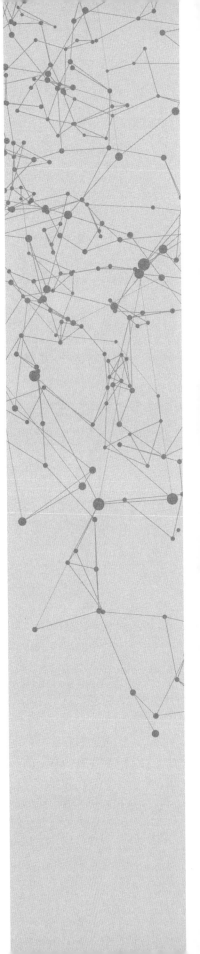

NOW Classrooms Series
Meg Ormiston et al.
This practical series presents classroom-tested lessons that educators can rely on to engage students in active learning, critical thinking, and problem solving. Use these lessons to connect technology to key learning outcomes and prepare learners to succeed in the 21st century.
BKF797, BKF798, BKF799, BKF800, BKF801

Designing Teacher-Student Partnership Classrooms
Meg Ormiston
Discover how teachers can become learning partners with their students. Cultivate a classroom environment in which students can apply what they've learned, teach it to their teacher and fellow students, and understand how their knowledge will be useful beyond the classroom.
BKF680

Create Future-Ready Classrooms, Now!
Meg Ormiston
Unite pedagogy and technology to inspire systemic school change. Explore digital tools that help seamlessly incorporate the technology-rich world into the classroom, understand how to use media for deeper learning, and examine a new approach to engagement and recognition.
BKF633

Creating a Digital-Rich Classroom
Meg Ormiston
Design and deliver standards-based lessons in which technology plays an integral role. This book provides a research base and practical strategies for using Web 2.0 tools to create engaging lessons that transform and enrich content.
BKF385

Solution Tree | Press
a division of
Solution Tree

Visit SolutionTree.com or call 800.733.6786 to order.